Imagining Mission with John V. Taylor

To all those who have been on this adventure of the imagination with us in our pioneering training over the last ten years, and to all those still to join in.

Imagining Mission with John V. Taylor

Cathy Ross and Jonny Baker

scm press

© Cathy Ross and Jonny Baker 2020

Published in 2020 by SCM Press
Editorial office
3rd Floor, Invicta House,
108–114 Golden Lane,
London EC1Y 0TG, UK

www.scmpress.co.uk

SCM Press is an imprint of Hymns Ancient & Modern Ltd
(a registered charity)

Hymns Ancient & Modern® is a registered trademark of
Hymns Ancient & Modern Ltd
13A Hellesdon Park Road, Norwich,
Norfolk NR6 5DR, UK

British Library Cataloguing in Publication data

A catalogue record for this book is available
from the British Library

ISBN 978-0-334-05950-9

Typeset by Regent Typesetting
Printed and bound by
CPI Group (UK) Ltd

Contents

Acknowledgements

There are various people we would like to thank. We are so grateful to Joanna Woodd, John Taylor's daughter, who gave Cathy the treasure trove of her father's travel diaries, which set us off on this journey of discovering more of Taylor's writings. We would also like to thank Emily Swan, who carefully scanned the diaries so that we could access them electronically. Thank you to John Chamberlain who photocopied the *CMS Newsletters* for me so that we could remove them from the Max Warren Collection in the Church Mission Society's Library.

Cathy would like to thank CMS and Ripon College Cuddesdon who agreed to her having study leave to focus on reading and sharing the material with Jonny. Thanks also to Ann Bartley and Judith Bright, the staff at Kinder Library, St John's College in Auckland, where she spent several weeks reading the material. Thank you both for the supply of excellent coffee and to Ann who lent her car to rescue the crucial notes that had been left behind! Thank you to Ken Osborne, CMS librarian in Oxford, for answering many questions and tracking down various sources for us. Finally, thank you to colleagues, students, friends and family who have listened to much of this material and, like us, have lived with John Taylor over the years.

Intro

Everything to Learn

The idea for this book was born after I read John Taylor's travel diaries. His daughter, Joanna Woodd, kindly gave them to me several years ago. I loved reading them. They are beautifully written and carefully crafted. They read more like a contemporary blog post than a mere list of names, dates and places. They are a fascinating mix of travelogue, political, social and cultural analysis and reportage, theological wonderings and spiritual reflections.

Taylor wrote these diaries when he was General Secretary of the Church Missionary Society (CMS) from 1963–74. There are eight of them and they act as a sort of aide-memoire to enable him to write his reports on his return.[1] Reading them took me into other worlds, they introduced me to people of different cultures who were living out their faith in so many different contexts, and sometimes the descriptions were so vivid and detailed that I felt as if I was there among them. Taylor also has a wonderful turn of phrase and is a master of metaphor, as you will discover. His writings reflect his own sympathy and empathy with local cultures, his own profound missiological insights, and his acute perception of the issues of the day. The diaries testify to his constant interest and fascination in the local culture and context. When in Pakistan, for example, he particularly requested to see a typical Pakistani film, the plot of which he describes in some detail in the diary and which he greatly enjoyed.[2] When in Japan, he wanted to see how Japanese young people spent their evenings so he and his companion went to a 'cellar coffee bar where kids in jeans and leather jackets were being entertained by a series of young beat groups'.[3] In Nigeria he attended a large open-air dance hall which was a popular spot in town.[4] In 1970 in Chicago he attended the musical *Hair*, which may have raised some eyebrows among more conservative CMS supporters.[5] He wrote thoughtfully about the impact the production had on him. These examples indicate his interest in popular culture and his curiosity about the world around him.

These experiences had an important influence on his thinking and writings, which are innovative and imaginative. He loved the arts and was a published poet and a musician. He was an improviser and a creative. His posture of humble listening, attentive curiosity and lively interest in the world around him made him an attractive person and mentor. This is what makes his writings so captivating and exciting for our day, over half a century later.

In his diaries, Taylor regularly referred to the *CMS Newsletter* that he was writing at the time. I knew about the *CMS Newsletters* but had not read many of them. They are a CMS 'institution', founded by a previous General Secretary, Wilson Cash (1926–41), and continued by Taylor's immediate predecessor, Max Warren (1942–63). They were a personal communication from the General Secretary to CMS members and anyone else who wished to subscribe. I wondered if I should read these as well, so I spent my last sabbatical immersing myself in them. Taylor wrote a total of 124 *CMS Newsletters* during his tenure as General Secretary and they are a treasure trove of missiology. They reflect Taylor's own missiological thinking, ideas and direction of travel. Essentially they are 1,500–2,000 words of accessible, current and creative missiological thinking and they always included a few reflections from his current reading that related to the topics addressed in the *Newsletter*.

During my sabbatical (in Aotearoa/New Zealand), I was sending photos of the exciting discoveries and new ideas in the *Newsletters* and diaries (72 photos in all!) to my colleague Jonny Baker, and we would have brief WhatsApp discussions, marvelling at the contemporary and challenging nature of Taylor's writings. On my return to England we decided to write this book together because we wanted to share what we had learned from John Taylor's creative wisdom and imaginative thinking. We have limited our reflection (mainly) to the *Newsletters* and travel diaries, although we have also invited other conversation partners to join the discussion. We are aware that Taylor has written much more, but we wanted to focus on this material, which is not so well known, as a springboard for reflecting on mission today.

We have loved delving into this material and have found so much of it challenging, innovative and pertinent for mission and theology in our day. By mission, we mean Taylor's own framing of mission: 'Mission means seeing what God is doing in a situation and trying to do it with him.'[6] Theology for Taylor is living, functional and practical. His ten years of teaching theology in the Lugandan language in Uganda (1945–54) forced him to think in concrete terms. He wrote of teaching during that time: 'This exercise instilled in me the realization that every abstract idea, including our idea of God, is derived from experience, and all revelation is given through things that happen. True theology has to be incarnational.'[7] This had a profound influence on his understanding of theology and mission. Theology is living and emerges out of a dynamic encounter with the world. In fact Taylor later asserts that there is no such thing as safe theology!

Taylor uses missiological and Christological lenses in his writings and reflections. Put simply, it is all about Jesus and it is all about mission. Taylor unpacks this in stimulating, challenging and sometimes provocative and risky ways. Clearly it was his involvement in mission and in CMS that enhanced and deepened his prophetic insights. He encourages us to develop a posture of imagination, innovation and improvisation in mission. These are qualities that Jonny and I have tried to promote and develop in our Pioneer Training at CMS over the last ten years. Indeed, it is Taylor who first encouraged us to see that 'the world through African eyes must involve this adventure of the imagination'.[8] This is what mission is all about – an adventure of the imagination, and that is what we explore in this book.

One of the inspiring things about Taylor's writing is his

boldness of speech. He has a freedom about him. It is not arrogant, but it does not feel as though he is overly concerned about what others might think. When Cathy was sending me photos of his newsletters from Aotearoa/New Zealand, I was preparing a paper on mission for a conference. And I found that, having read John Taylor, I was inspired to be free, to speak from the heart, to speak boldly. We have tried to carry that voice into this book and hope that you might experience the same emboldening through reading it.

The book is divided into three sections: Church, Mission, Society. These are the most common themes that emerge in Taylor's writings. We decided to share the writing of this book between us, so we have written three chapters each. Jonny writes about church, Cathy writes about mission and we both contribute to the section on society, with Jonny writing about the environment and Cathy writing on other faiths.

Imagination, or the ability to imagine, is a red thread that runs throughout the book. Jonny tries to imagine what church could be in this new era and plays with various ideas and metaphors to explore this. His opening gambit is 'imagine if church were not the point of church' – now there is a challenge! The second chapter in this section is about training and is entitled 'Christ the Innovator', an expression from Taylor. Here he riffs off Taylor, imagining training as innovation and not for 'academic ostriches'. He explores the turn to context and how training needs to become unstuck and freed from the domination of Western methods and content.

Cathy explores what it means for mission to be an adventure of the imagination. Mission is local, mission costs us everything, mission is dangerous, and mission is joining in with God, are some of the ideas explored here. The second chapter explores the continuing need for mission organizations. She draws on Taylor's wisdom to discuss how an institution can remain a movement, continue to ask risky questions and reframe power as humility. This is helped by rejecting the settler impulse.

In the section on society Jonny explores Taylor's prophetic and prescient reflections on environmental issues. Taylor's phrase 'Enough is Enough' is a powerful and appropriate message for our indulgent Western society. Jonny provides a brief analysis of our current lamentable state concerning the environment and then offers some ways forward based on Taylor's analysis of the theology of enough. He also draws on other contemporary thinkers and writers to offer a hopeful way forward.

Cathy then reflects on multi-faith relations, drawing on Taylor's ideas of Jesus as 'the great disturber' who challenges so many of our preconceived ideas and theories. Taylor does not duck the hard issues of the uniqueness of Christ and the way of the cross but forces us to think more expansively about these and other issues.

Imagination can be helped by paying attention to processes of creativity. To that end we have added a reflection on creativity at the end of each chapter. These are also accompanied by some exercises to help you flex your own creative muscle. While there is something mysterious about creativity, ideas and imagination, they can also be cultivated through practice. Jonny concludes with an Outro where he reflects further on the theme of imagination. Our hope is that this book will spark your imagination in the way that it has ours. We have resisted providing pragmatic solutions, preferring to leave the imaginative work to the reader.

We hope you will enjoy what you discover here. We have been excited, enlivened and enriched by our conversation with John Taylor. His is the kind of missiology that we endeavour to embody and live out. His original mind and fresh ideas have sparked so many thoughts and ideas about mission. He has been a hugely influential figure for CMS and we find ourselves drawing on his missiology as we think about what it means to be engaged in mission in the twenty-first century. In mission we are always learning, making mistakes and learning all over again. John Taylor expressed this well; may we emulate this sentiment as we try to witness to Jesus in all our various contexts: 'I shall come as a stranger with everything to learn again.'[9]

Notes

1 Travel Diaries: Sierra Leone and Nigeria 1960; USA and Mexico 1963; Iran, Egypt, Jordan and Israel 1964; Malaya, Hong Kong, Japan and New York, 1965; Australasia, 1966; Pakistan, Nepal, Afghanistan, Moscow, 1968; Ceylon, North India (incomplete), 1969; USA, 1970.

2 Travel Diary, Pakistan, Nepal, Afghanistan, Moscow, 1968. Clarkabad, Pakistan, Wednesday 27 November 1968, p. 138.

3 Travel Diary, Malaya, Hong Kong, Japan, New York 1965. Tokyo, Wednesday 3 March 1965, p. 62.

4 Travel Diary, West Africa, 1960. Lagos, Saturday 2 April 1960, p. 173.

5 Travel Diary, USA 1970. Chicago, Wednesday 15 April 1970, p. 49.

6 CMS Newsletter, No. 382, June 1974. The CMS Newsletters and his travel diaries are deposited in the Max Warren Collection at CMS in Oxford.

7 John V.Taylor, 'My Pilgrimage in Mission', International Bulletin of Missionary Research, April 1993, pp. 59–60.

8 John V. Taylor, The Primal Vision, Christian Presence Amid African Religion (London: SCM Press, 1963), p. 41.

9 Travel Diary, West Africa, 1960, p. 177.

PART ONE

Church

I

Leap Over the Wall or Perish[1]

Imagine that church is not the point of church

Rather, church exists to participate in the healing of all things – the world, its peoples, the planet itself. That is the point. Church is God's people participating in that liberation, a communion in mission. Church is Christ's body prolonging the logic of the mission and ministry of Jesus Christ in the world. That's why John Taylor says that the world is 'the church's milieu'.[2] If you had a blank sheet of paper and could design church with that purpose in mind, and anything is possible, what would you come up with?[3] Fresh imagination is required because we seem to have got stuck. You might also agree that we need to leap over walls that we have created, in order to be in the world.

Imagine that church is like yeast

To make a starter or culture for sourdough bread you mix flour and water together and leave it for 24 hours and then repeat each day. After about four or five days the mixture starts to bubble and the natural yeast has been activated. You then add some of this starter to flour, water and salt each time you want to make a loaf of bread. Mix it and leave it and it will rise if you are using a no-knead recipe, or kneading will encourage the yeast to activate and the dough will rise faster. Wild yeast is magical, it is all around us, invisible, an agent waiting to be activated. When a loaf of bread has been made the yeast becomes one with the bread, no longer a separate thing. But it affects the whole. Without it the bread would be flat. Jesus likened the kingdom of God to yeast. If the milieu of the Church is the world then church as yeast is an exciting picture. Initially it is separate but through close proximity becomes a transforming agent that is also changed itself in the process of making something good and new and wonderful in the world.

Imagine that church is like a forest[4]

A forest is an environment teeming with abundant life appropriate to the part of the world it is in – trees, shrubs, plants, fungi, birds, animals, insects, bugs, butterflies. A healthy, biodiverse woodland or forest flourishes with multiple layers or storeys and a diversity of species. There are ancient big trees at the top of the canopy – standards like oaks or beech or ash soaking in the light. There is a middle layer or understorey of hazel or hawthorn, for example, and then at ground level shrubs, ferns and smaller plants that appear in different seasons. There are different mixes of trees in different parts of the forest. To regenerate a forest, light is the key. Light can be let in through thinning or making a clearing. When that happens what seemed dormant suddenly bursts into life. Because there is a seedbank in the soil and seeds that have blown on the wind or been redistributed by animals (through bird droppings for example or squirrels burying nuts) you don't even need to plant things.

It is also possible to manage the forest by planting wisely. Diversity is important because if you have a monoculture you risk losing everything if a disease or pest attacks. You don't want just big trees – the diversity is of size as well as variety. The forest is an environment that is abundant rather than scarce – one beech tree can produce 30,000 seeds and so much life can emerge from the soil.[5] Things don't last for ever and when trees die they seed other things or as they rot become habitats for insects. Everything in the forest is interconnected and interdependent – one thing affects another and in many ways they need one another. Recent research has shown how trees are social beings.[6]

By 'imagining church as forest' we do not mean 'a church' but everything that is connected to Christ and communicates Christ. This environment would include denominations, festivals, bookshops, retreat centres, podcasts and their associated communities. Standards at the top of the tree canopy might be a big city centre church, a cathedral, a festival, a mission organization, a podcast, a church network or a retreat centre. Then there are lots of mid-size trees such as congregations, a bookshop, a website, a youth network, an app. Finally, there are many small ones – people meeting in ones and twos, sharing meals in homes, a parent and toddler group, spiritual direction, or praying via a Whatsapp group.

The environment is abundant. The seeds of the Gospel are in multiple places; if you were to make a clearing it is a safe bet that something new would be seeded. The wider environment of church will flourish if it is as diverse as a forest and if there are clearings from time to time. Growth is not a technical or mechanical process of models that can be delivered. It is more likely to take place by paying attention to what's going on, working with what's there, and trying to add diversity or reintroduce some ancient species. And the more interdependent it is the better.

Leadership is more like woodland management or gardening. God is at work regenerating in surprising places. What is critical is to let God's light in – God must be central. A denomination is part of the forest, a large congregation part of the ecology that can be a great gift for seeding other things. But the forest is by no means simply big churches – that would be a poor environment. It is tempting for big churches to think it's all about them and sometimes other parts of the forest are invisible to them. But so much of church is meeting in small groups, in homes, in coffee shops, online in ways that are invisible. Two thirds of the Church ecosystem in the West does not even gather in congregations. People navigate church very differently from how they used to, perhaps due to the possibilities afforded by communication through digital media. It is possible, for example, to have attended something big or middling for a season and then be in a small group and resourced through a phone app, a festival and a community online gathered around a podcast. This is all part of the forest. Parts of church die – they have their seasons and that is all good. They can seed other things and in dying create space for newness to emerge. Life teems in all sorts of places and especially at the edges between things, a key insight from permaculture.

Imagine church is something you leave after a while

This may sound shocking but research in the Western world shows that this is true for the majority of Christians.[7] This is usually described negatively – people have backslidden or lost their faith, for example. But the research shows a very different picture. People leave for multiple reasons and often it is because their faith has developed or matured or become more expansive. They leave for the sake of mission or their own growth. They leave to connect more with the world. They have been parented and grown up and are ready to serve Christ in the world.[8] Of course they haven't really left in that sense. There is an issue of language – we tend to use the word 'church' to describe a building or congregation. But they are part of God's people and are connecting to Christ and others in the body of Christ beyond attendance at a Sunday gathering.

If church exists for the sake of the world, then imagining church as having a season of maturing as a disciple and being part of a close-knit community but with an expectation to move out into mission after several years, makes formation sound like a really good thing. If that was deemed to be acceptable, it would be healthy to keep a connection and to come back to be resourced and encouraged or to see someone for spiritual direction. Perhaps in this new space they might meet with a small community in a home, with a mix of Christians and seekers joining to create something good locally. This would resemble the religious orders that spread out in mission from a community base, or a minster model of church. There is an old adage that if you take a piece of coal out of the fire and put it on the hearth it burns out. This used to be a warning to go to church regularly. But in today's environment this adage is no longer true. You can remain connected with others in all sorts of spaces apart from the organized, congregational models of church.

One of the significant changes that digital communication has made is the assumption that we can always connect to information and to other people wherever we are. This seems a healthy assumption to bring to relationship with God and others in the body of Christ – we are always connected, always on, rather than church being the connection once or twice a week. One of the challenges of the new environment in which people are making faith and church differently is that you need a rich environment. So, coming back to the forest imagery, we really want, for example, committed Jesuits to run a retreat centre and share the gift of Ignatian spirituality. We want the Nomad podcast to produce really good in-depth interviews with theologians exploring Christianity in today's world so that others can access the content and talk about it.[9] We want cathedrals to keep the tradition of choral music and their wonderful space so that others can visit and worship. So the more wandering type of pilgrim needs others who inhabit particular traditions and spaces with depth and authenticity.

Contemporary Western society has very much placed a free-choosing self at the centre of things. It can easily become my choosing what and whom to connect with, when I choose. This is quite a contrast to the discipline of committed discipleship in community. Church is the network of Christ in this space and people are navigating it very differently. Our observation is that those who have left traditional models are as committed to exploring faith and the journey of discipleship as those that remain. Rather than see it as a problem, perhaps it can be an environment in which there is connection, and in which gifts can be exchanged. The challenge for any part of the forest of church is to have something to contribute, something that seeds life wherever it is in the forest and whatever type of tree or plant it is. It is a dynamic, fluid and organic church that is alive and moves and changes. It is brought into being by the Spirit who is also alive and dynamic and at work in the world. A combination of faithful and creative participation and prayerful discernment of what the Spirit is doing is a good blend.

Imagine church is like a nursery

Thinking about leaving church after maturing in faith led us to imagine church as like a greenhouse or garden nursery, where there is a protected space and good care for vulnerable seeds and plants that are young and small and at risk from adverse weather conditions. In a nursery they can be tended regularly, fed and watered and enabled to grow until they are strong enough to be planted out. That is always a risky moment – are they strong enough, are they ready? Sometimes they can be taken outside and brought back in a few times to get them hardier before that transition. But how might we view church and our involvement in it if it was a place to grow and mature and deepen roots but with the knowledge that you would be moving to a tougher environment in due course, to live out discipleship in the world? This is not for everyone. For some, becoming mature might mean being in a ministry in one of the churches that nurtures others. John Taylor describes church as a house that will provide shelter, recognizing that people need care; his concern is that it should not be shut away from the world.[10]

Imagine church as lots of little congregations

Research into 'Fresh Expressions of Church in England' named its report 'The Day of Small Things'.[11] This is because so many of the new things are small in size. The majority fall within the range of 15–55 people. Small might be five or six gathered around a meal table on a week night, a local messy church, or a monthly gathering exploring faith in the outdoors. Small has advantages – it has a lighter touch in terms of structures and flexibility. It makes innovation and experimentation easier. It's much easier to build community because everyone can know and relate to everyone else. It also has its challenges because the traditional assumptions of a building and a paid minister supported by a congregation do not make sense for a small congregation. John Taylor was writing before Fresh Expressions but it sometimes feels as though he saw what was coming.[12] One theme he regularly came back to was 'little congregations', which he saw as the most important unit and critical to the life of the Church. Depending on their culture and circumstances, these little congregations will be translated for the local context and look different in form and function. They think about the life of their local community around them and shape their meeting and involvements accordingly.[13]

The small congregations are not sub-churches or a half-way house through which people will eventually be drawn into 'real' or 'proper' church (by which people usually mean the main congregation on a Sunday). This always used to be an issue in youth work and probably still is. There was an expectation that you would do really creative things with young people in small groups but eventually they would join the real thing, and of course they rarely did unless they were familiar with church already! The little congregations are not interim structures that will eventually grow into parish churches. At times it may be right for this to happen, but it does not have to work this way. In the report *Mission Shaped Church*,[14] Rowan Williams helpfully used the phrase 'mixed economy of church', recognizing that the wider household of the Church can have a mix of traditional models alongside new and different expressions. Picking up on our earlier metaphor it's all part of the wider ecosystem of the forest. Not everything has to become an oak tree.

The Church of England created a new piece of legislation, a Bishop's Mission Order, so that something other than a parish church can be part of that mixed economy. In practice this has subsequently proved difficult to move into the wider structures of the Church. This is due to the legacy of the structures but also to a culture that is often resistant to a process of change. The Church often seems to regard any other form than the conventional parish congregation as subnormal and peripheral.[15] On a more positive note, one of the surprising things in the 'Day of Small Things' research was how many Fresh Expressions have a relationship with a congregation or parish church that seeded them, either through a person sent or a team, as a new congregation, or sometimes a request to come under their umbrella. The parish could be reconceived as a hub for little congregations or Fresh Expressions, but what would it look like if the little congregations were seen as the most important unit because they are where the life and dynamism is?[16] There is talk in the Church of England at the moment of 'resource churches'. This generally means a large city-centre church with lots of young adults which then plants out other churches. In some cases that has happened really well – for example St Peter's in Brighton. A parish as a hub for seeding lots of little congregations could be another kind of resource church.

There are four different aspects of Christian life and witness that these small groups could include in their life – reflection, service, worship and evangelism – in order to be healthy, local expressions of church. It is vital for Christians everywhere to reflect together on their own context, what is happening in the world around them, to be guided by the Holy Spirit to see what God is doing in their context, and to understand their calling and responsibility as God's people in the world.

Discipleship is a buzz word at the moment and is seen to be the solution to the Church's challenges. Groups are the ideal spaces in which to discuss and interchange ideas and learn together and lean into the questions of people in the group. Theology and discipleship come alive as people take responsibility for their faith together and move away from being passive adherents, which is what can happen so easily in large congregations.[17] Independent thought and approaches to truth are welcomed in this environment. This can feel very different from larger environments where theology seems to be defended and truth becomes a party line. It is extraordinary in this day and age how many churches continue with sermons as unquestioned monologues from the pulpit.[18]

Discussion must be earthed in the local. Taylor says, 'Every unit of Christian Presence in the world should find its identity primarily in its missionary concern for that area of life towards which its members are immediately responsible.'[19] This is what we would now describe as a small missional community. To illustrate the basic level of questions we might be asking, he gives the example of a group of factory workers from Madras (now Chennai). This group of factory workers started by describing their job, then asked if how they did their job made any difference to others, then what they earned and whether that was fair and whether they worked enough to earn their salary. These are basic questions about the significance of work, the nature of relationships, the world of industry and, eventually, where God is at work. So much talk in church is too theoretical or abstract.[20]

The Bible is a key resource for such groups and for mission and must be read with reference to our contemporary lives and the world around us. It is helpful if it is opened up in ways other than an expert sharing in great detail what it means. Practices such as *lectio divina* or dwelling in the word, or Ignatian imaginative reading, or simply asking great questions on a passage, might be some approaches to try. Reading attentively in this way can be challenging, confronting and transforming. God speaks! We can listen politely to a sermon but when confronted with the biblical text it is harder to avoid the demands placed upon our lives. Individualistic piety can be avoided by insisting that the group's reflection leads to some form of active service. This prevents the group from becoming introverted and self-indulgent. A healthy group moves between reflection and service. Reflection fuels service and service drives a deeper search for the meaning of the Gospel and discipleship.[21]

Church regulations can be so frustrating for groups like this, depending on your tradition or denomination. Sacramental worship is usually only allowed to be experienced at the centre, controlled by the priesthood. It's hard to see that changing any time soon, though we would welcome lay presidency. And yet if groups discover a sacramental life they can take on greater responsibility for a healing and gospel-bearing church in that place.[22] Groups tend to find ways round this either through the local bishop turning a blind eye, through explicit permission to experiment, or through finding legitimate hacks of the system's code. Pressure will surely lead to changes here. In rural areas the ordained can be servicing multiple communities in unsustainable ways. The Church of England is a lot looser round the edges now than it used to be, and indeed than it was in John Taylor's day, but there is a whole lot more loosening that could be done.

If these small groups are to be the growing edge of the Church, they must not be for believers only. We should expect to find unbelieving friends and colleagues welcome and in debate over a Bible passage and current issues. The Church must be welcoming to all, but a welcome poster or desk in a church does not really do it for the person seeking, for whom what goes on inside is absolutely foreign.[23] Meeting round a meal table with friends is surely an easier place to connect. It is in the small group that one can feel at home and belong without first having to make a commitment.

Imagine church is more a movement than an institution

It is easy to say something like this and it sounds as if institutions are therefore a problem. They are not. We need them. They can be a great gift. So the Church will have institutional form, except when it is very new in a context, but the critical thing is this is not what makes it the Church.[24] The institutional form is incidental and, throughout history, as the movement progresses the form will and can change and adapt. It's alive, it's a body, indwelt by the creative Spirit of God. Tradition is similar. There is great gift in the past and in tradition, great wells and treasures. But when it becomes stuck or absolutized it can become a heavy weight that crushes the life out of initiatives. It's helpful to remember that tradition is something living that moves and changes according to the times and cultures and contexts, and to what the Spirit is saying.

Imagine church as fringe-dwellers

Jesus was loved by outsiders, fringe-dwellers. He spent time with them, seemed particularly drawn to them, and was definitely good news for them. He went to the other side of the lake to free a man who lived in the tombs and was tormented in his mind by unclean spirits. He touched unclean lepers and allowed himself to be touched by an unclean woman who had been bleeding for years. He stopped to notice beggars and to restore their sight, but also to make them seen by those who refused to see them. He built his team out of uneducated working-class men. He loved women and seemed able to lift their burden of shame. He gravitated to fringe places – the wilderness, a well in Samaria, the other side of the lake, tax collectors' homes, the North. He taught that a life that is full is one that is poor, grief-stricken, persecuted, peace-making, hungry for, and yielded to, God's way. The Church is Jesus' body and Jesus' community of friends. So she is surely most herself when she is at the periphery with those who are fringe-dwellers.[25]

Both Jonny and Cathy are involved in training and encouraging pioneer ministry. It's been really encouraging to find that so many pioneers see those at the fringes who are often unseen or unnoticed by others and then build something with them. The Spirit is the one who prompts and calls them there and God is the one who builds the Church. It's hard because there are not a lot of resources or visible signs of success. In the wider church it sometimes feels as if the good desire for growth distorts things by looking for success at the centre where it is easier to get quick results, rather than at the fringes. But we love it that the Church at her best – when she is herself – will always go to the edges and be joined by fringe-dwellers.

Becoming unstuck

There are many more imaginings possible. We teach students who are training for leadership as pioneers or as ordinands in the Church of England and have become convinced that using our imagination is perhaps the biggest challenge. All of our imaginations are more colonized than we like to think. We think in particular ways about church, in patterns that can be quite stuck. There are several ways that stuckness manifests itself in relation to church. We outline a few of these below. These are deliberately at the end of the chapter because we wanted to focus on creative possibilities, but it is important to hold a mirror up to ourselves as church so that we can really see what is going on. Indeed, John Taylor writes with shocking boldness about church and the Church of England in particular.

Church has become too introverted. Church is too focused on itself and its internal workings. If you are a keen Christian the chances are you will be encouraged to give more and more time to church activities rather than to living life in the world. There is an obsession with cultic activities like sermons and worship leading. People then develop a religious sweet tooth so that they love to hear more sermons and sing more worship songs. Church can often mutate into a worship club that exists to keep its members happy, 'owning its own premises and employing a full-time official to run it just as if it were a tennis club or a learned society'.[26] John Taylor's way of putting it is that it is wrongly focused on services rather than service.[27]

Church is socially constructed. It is something people make and have made in response to particular times and places, as their way of working out what it means to be the body of Christ. They make it with cultural things – music, words, architecture, ritual structures, leadership, governance, money flows and so on. This construction is informed by reflection on the tradition, on the Scriptures and on the times, the context. There are many constructions possible and World Christianity shows us that many exist within the global ecosystem of the Church. This is the gift of other cultures – they show us that what we thought was the way of doing things is simply a local theology, and they bring a redemptive gift that we have not seen before.

Parishes, church buildings, bishops, regulations – these are things people have made up; Anglican episcopacy is the product of culture and history rather than theology.[28] The Church did fine without a parish system for 1,000 years or more.[29] That is not to say that things that have been constructed should be taken lightly or that they are not good things. But it does mean they can be unmade too. And new things can be made that suit other local cultures. Indeed, the question of translation into local culture is a critical question in mission. The Church must recognize the necessity to reformulate her faith, her praying, her worship and her community engagement, as well as her social and prophetic dimensions, in ways and language accessible to each local culture. The imposition of Western liturgies and ways of doing things has been debated in the Anglican Communion and has resulted in recognizing that creative inculturation is at the heart of good practice and to be encouraged globally.[30] But equally, each generation needs a new translation of these things, as well as a way of connecting with the global Church. CMS has nearly always held up the goal of mission being indigenous, or a local church led by local people. Henry Venn was famously the great proponent of that in the early nineteenth century. The forms of church are as much an issue of translation as the gospel message. That is as true in our own context and culture as it is for mission across cultures. We have seen huge changes in the wider culture in the last 50 years and many of the ways in which church has previously been made are creaking at the edges. The challenge is that ways of doing things get absolutized and then stuck, rather than translated afresh for each new era or generation.

Those with power like things the way they are because they are doing well out of business as usual. Buildings are one powerful example – when most people hear the word 'church', they think of an old building with rows of benches facing towards the front. But there is great freedom in Christ and the Spirit is beckoning the Church to the edges, to new forms, to new imaginings and embodiments, new architecture, new translations.

Steve Collins has brought wonderful imagination to thinking about the kinds of architecture used in church spaces and how these might be reimagined. Rather than church being like the throne room, classroom or court, what would it look like as a living room with hospitality, openness and availability being core values?[31] The last decades have seen encouraging innovation through the Emerging Church and Fresh Expressions of Church, often through small things done with fringe-dwellers, which has been a sign of great hope.

The Church of England's way of making church has led to the Church being associated with the middle classes, with wealth, power and establishment. Taylor supports the Church losing her favoured status.[32] This would then enable the Church to become a servant people and to discard the status of privilege that is to be found at the centre. He suggests that the Church needs to get off its high horse and muck in; and he is referring to the Church of England.[33] The buildings that are monuments to Christendom and the accompanying livery alienate many people. Bishops live in palaces – what sort of sign and message is that to the wider culture, when we have the good news that Jesus is alongside the poor and broken? Taylor abhors what he names the 'stultifying and repressive effect of Christian respectability' that kills a dynamic spirit of love and acceptance.[34] This is the other side of loving and practical service. The Christian Church could be a healing community offering a creative and healing love, but so often we are marked by a narrow spirit of conformity that encourages good behaviour rather than this dynamic spirit of love and welcome.

If one response to the word 'church' is to picture a building, the second most common is to imagine a congregation of people gathered into one place worshipping – usually in that building. One of the words translated as church in the New Testament, *ekklesia*, means 'the gathered' so there is a place for that. However, it has become so dominant that many of the other ways of being church have become invisible. This is back to the forest imagery – if we could imagine a much richer ecosystem perhaps we could let go of these two pictures as the only ways to imagine church.

Whatever else it is or isn't, church is people. And crucially it is all God's people. The word sometimes used for people is 'lay', from the Greek *laos*, meaning people generally. Everyone is lay, including those who are ordained. Church is the people of God, people following in the way of Christ, a people in mission, a pilgrim people, a people scattered abroad. It is a lay movement. All of us, every single member, every single part, is precious and valuable whether it looks important or not and together we make up Christ's body in the world. In the 1970s, when there was a wave of renewal in the Church that seemed to loosen the dominant clerical paradigm of the time, one of the phrases used was 'body ministry'. This was an exciting recognition that everyone is involved and has a part to play, not just the clergy. Looking back, it was very focused on church-y activities, so it would be good to move that into discipleship in the local workplace and family and neighbourhood. The role of the ordained then is to enable the body to participate in God's mission, to enable lay ministry in the world which is the milieu of the Church.[35]

Imagine church is risk-taking and free

Reading the book of Acts is breathtaking. Here the Church is hardly able to catch breath to keep up with the dynamic explosion of growth as the news of Jesus' life, death and resurrection ripples outwards from Jerusalem along the trade routes of the Roman Empire, and new communities form. There is no settling down – the Spirit beckons the apostles across borders they thought were uncrossable – to Samaritans, eunuchs, gentiles – and it gradually dawns on them that God is the God of the whole world, of all peoples and is concerned for the redemption of all things and all peoples. And this God is free, not contained by their religion or denomination or theology but always ahead, moving beyond. We follow this risk-taking God and where God's Spirit is, there is freedom.[36] So imagine being part of that God's community, risk-taking and free.

Exercising Creativity

There are no rules

Creativity is often thought of as a gift – you either have it or you don't. And more often than not people say they don't! However, it's more helpful to think of it as like a muscle that can be exercised. Without use it can go flabby, but through regular use it is strengthened. To help exercise that creative muscle we offer a reflection on imagination at the end of each chapter, with some suggestions to get your creative juices flowing in relation to the theme of the chapter.

Over the years Jonny has collected a number of books on creativity and how artists think. One of the things they have in common is that they all stress the importance of not following rules,[37] or that there are no rules.[38] Whatever you think, think the opposite.[39] Challenge your assumptions.[40] If everyone else zigs, then zag.[41] Break the rules![42]

We think in patterns and once our brain has developed a pattern it's simplest just to go back to that pattern again and again. It saves energy and effort. Imagination requires being whacked off course, being interrupted and jolted away from our usual way of looking at things. Then we might discover the art of looking sideways, we might imagine a different possibility. This requires an ability to suspend our usual judgements about things, what we assume is normal or common sense. Those judgements can act as both defences and filters: rejecting new ideas or filtering them out without giving them a second thought.

This is challenging for Christians because we have largely been schooled to think that following the rules is the right thing to do and that there is a right answer. The unspoken assumption can be that the way things are done is also backed up by God and the Bible, so it's quite a big deal to question things! Furthermore, churches have lots of people who are quite good at judging whether things are right or wrong and they can feel threatened by people asking awkward questions. So it is genuinely hard to suspend your judgement. Critical thinking is important, but not when you need to be coming up with ideas. Edward de Bono, one of the developers of the idea of lateral thinking, devised a tool for groups called the Six Thinking Hats.[43] To separate out the parts of a thinking process he would get the group to put on a particular hat for the kind of thinking they were engaging in at any time. For example, the white hat is for facts, the black hat for caution, the green hat for exploration and new ideas. So when a group is exploring new ideas with the green hat, judgement on them is suspended until a different hat is worn, which is usually later in the process. You might need to use this sort of process with a particular group you are working with.

Exercises

1 One way of thinking imaginatively about church is to identify and name some of the assumptions and rules, or even some of the sacred cows, that exist. They are most likely unspoken. For example, an unspoken rule might be that you must go to church because if you don't your faith will die out; or that church needs an employed minister; or that church has to meet in a special building; or that worship involves singing and preaching. And so on...

Write these unspoken rules down on pieces of paper. Then with a small group of friends over a meal or at the pub explore what would happen if you broke those rules and see where this leads you in your thinking. This exercise in exploration will lead you towards discovering new ideas. It doesn't necessarily mean that you will abandon a particular rule, though you may. To give an example, when Jonny was on a retreat in Ireland, the group visited a lot of small churches that were in ruins, with the roof open to the sky. They often reflected and prayed together in those spaces, which prompted the thought of how good it was to meet outdoors, open to the sky, and how accessible that is for most people's experience of wonder. Now, through Forest Church and other such explorations, many groups are meeting as church in the outdoors without a building. Grace, the community that Jonny is part of, did not meet in the church building for six months last summer. That is one example of where not following the rule of meeting in a church building can lead.

2 Take John Taylor's phrase about church having to 'leap over the wall or perish' and explore what church might look like if we assumed that presence in the community meant participating in life rather than being shut away in a building. Similarly, take his thought that the church did fine without the parish system for 1,000 years or more. Slay that sacred cow and see where that leads you in your thinking.

3 Take the subheadings throughout the chapter as provocations that you might like to follow and see what happens if you do. For example, take the sub-heading 'Imagine church is like a forest'. Get a large sheet of paper and draw a forest to represent church either in your area or in the wider ecosystem. What are the standards, the shrubs, the understory? Is it diverse? What is missing in the ecosystem? If you were a woodland manager what might you add? Or where would you make a clearing? Where does that lead you? What do you notice?

Notes

1 *CMS Newsletter*, No. 275, October 1964.

2 *CMS Newsletter*, No. 267, January 1964.

3 Travel Diary, USA and Mexico, 1963, p. 76. Taylor says we need new metaphors to explain the relationship between God, the Church and the world. So we have come up with a few.

4 Taylor uses arboreal imagery. See *CMS Newsletter*, No. 285, September 1965.

5 Peter Wohlleben, *The Hidden Life of Trees* (London: William Collins, 2017), p. 29.

6 Wohlleben, *The Hidden Life of Trees*, p. 29.

7 One example of this is research in Scotland by Steve Aisthorpe, documented in his *The Invisible Church* (Edinburgh: Saint Andrew Press, 2016), where he shows that twice as many practising Christians don't attend church as do. This would be replicated in England, North America, Canada and so on.

8 John V. Taylor, *A Church Reshaped* (London: CMS, 1975). Taylor suggests that if we are to be where Jesus calls us to be, alongside those in the world, it may mean leaving the church – as you might leave a parent to whom you owe existence itself.

9 www.nomadpodcast.co.uk/.

10 *CMS Newsletter*, No. 267, January 1964.

11 A report produced by the Church Army Research Unit in 2016 – see www.churcharmy.org/Publisher/File.aspx?ID=204265 (accessed 10.8.2019).

12 *CMS Newsletter*, No. 308, October 1967. By way of example, in the late 1960s, aware of changes in society – such as both partners working and the weekend being important leisure time, Taylor was beginning to question just how fit for purpose the parish system was. He asks pointedly, 'What should a missionary Church be doing in Britain, Sunday by Sunday, for the tens of thousands who stream in their cars to the coast and the countryside? Try to cajole them into postponing their trip till midday in order to attend their parish churches first? Or try to coax them into a parish church at the other end of their journey? Or try to legislate so that as few amenities as possible will be available to them, in the hope of discouraging the Sunday exodus altogether?' He comments that none of these ideas would occur to us in a 'non-christian culture'. It would not enter our minds to consider how to draw people into church buildings; rather we would be considering how to witness in a relevant way.

13 *CMS Newsletter*, No. 308, October 1967.

14 Graham Cray (ed.), *Mission Shaped Church* (London: Church House Publishing, 2004).

15 *CMS Newsletter*, No. 308, October 1967.

16 *CMS Newsletter*, No. 308.

17 John V. Taylor, *Rosewindow* 8, 1975, pp. i–ii.

18 *CMS Newsletter*, No. 309, November 1967.

19 Taylor, *A Church Reshaped*, p. 13.

20 *A Church Reshaped*, p. 13.

21 *A Church Reshaped*, p. 13.

22 *CMS Newsletter*, No. 311, December 1967.

23 *CMS Newsletter*, No. 311.

24 Travel Diary, Iran, Egypt, Jordan, Israel, 1964, p. 102.

25 *A Church Reshaped*, p. 10. Taylor commends the image of the Christian as a fringe-dweller.

26 *A Church Reshaped*, p. 8.

27 *CMS Newsletter*, No. 308, October 1967.

28 *CMS Newsletter*, No. 386, November 1974.

29 *CMS Newsletter*, No. 386.

30 David Holeton (ed.), *Liturgical Inculturation in the Anglican Communion: York Statement 'Down to Earth Worship'* (Cambridge: Grove series, Ridley Hall, 1989), p. 6.

31 Steve Collins, in *Future Present* (Proost, 2018).

32 *CMS Newsletter*, No. 333, December 1969.

33 *CMS Newsletter*, No. 283, June 1965.

34 *CMS Newsletter*, No. 283, June 1965.

35 *CMS Newsletter*, No. 353, October 1971.

36 Travel Diary, Iran, Egypt, Jordan, Israel, 1964, p. 102.

37 Roger Von Oech, *A Whack on the Side of the Head* (New York, NY: Warner Books, 1983), has 'follow the rules' as one of his mental blocks to creative thinking.

38 John Hegarty, *Hegarty On Creativity: There Are No Rules* (London: Thames & Hudson, 2014).

39 Paul Arden, *Whatever You Think Think the Opposite* (London: Penguin Books, 2006).

40 Alan Fletcher, *The Art of Looking Sideways* (London: Phaidon Press, 2001), p. 29.

41 Hegarty, *On Creativity*, p. 42.

42 Will Gompertz, *Think Like an Artist* (London: Penguin Random House, 2015), p. 190.

43 Edward de Bono, *Teach Your Child to Think* (London: Penguin Books, 1993), p. 74.

2

In the Name of Christ
the Innovator

Imagine training for the whole people of God

This chapter is really part two of the previous chapter and an attempt to deepen and build on the imagining begun there. To recap, church is essentially a lay movement, a spread-out people participating in the mission of God, which is the healing of all things. Its milieu is the world. It is a much wider and deeper ecosystem than simply buildings, congregations and institutions. It is Christ's body in the world joining in with what God is doing and sharing the good news about Jesus Christ. The great thing about most laity is that they are already embedded in the secular world through their work and life. How then might the Church encourage, equip and train people for participation, service, mission and ministry in the world?

As part of the Church the calling of lay people is primarily to work in the world and not the Church. They are yeast and salt. So training for them is about being resourced and connected but in ways that enable them to have free agency in the world to fulfil God's call as teachers, artists, cleaners, businesswomen, builders, app designers, farmers and so on. That mission is not to be collapsed into a spiritual compartment of life – behaving nicely by not stealing pencils, and witnessing to colleagues in natural ways. Those are both basic things but very reductionist if that's all discipleship means. The community Jonny is part of created a mission noticeboard that had every member of the church on it with what they did that was good in the world. For most the biggest thing was their work but they were also involved in charitable activities, local community engagement, parenting, giving, being a carer. What was extraordinary was that this noticeboard made visible a huge engagement in mission that was previously hidden, and is probably hidden in most churches. Usually a church mission noticeboard is reserved for missionaries overseas and full-time Christian workers. We have to orient our understanding of mission and discipleship beyond church ministry and church-y activities and train people to be whole-life disciples. We do need some who will volunteer time and energy in church ministry, so that it can resource and encourage the whole people of God in their wider mission, but we trust that God distributes gifts as the Spirit wills.

A subset of the laity are those called to some sort of leadership in the Church, whether as pioneers, lay ministers or ordained. How do we imagine those roles in today's Church? What sort of training might equip them to navigate the challenges and lead the whole people of God creatively into the future, setting God's people free? John Taylor thought a profound review of clergy training was needed because, in his opinion, one of the primary functions of a clergyperson is to enable lay people to witness in their own contexts.[1]

Imagine training for an adventure

One of our favourite phrases of John Taylor's is from his book *The Primal Vision* where he describes mission as 'an adventure of the imagination'.[2] He suggests that if the task of translation into the African worldview was really taken to its logical conclusion, the results might be unrecognizable because they were so inside the African worldview. The diagram below is a model for reflective mission practice that conveys this idea and what might be involved in it.

There is a creative interplay between who the student is and the context they are in (you in context), the church tradition they are part of (church), the resources in theology and mission

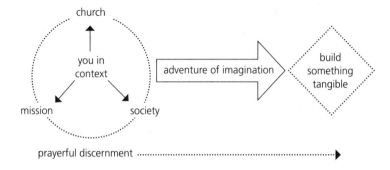

they can draw on (mission), and the culture they are in and what is going on in the world (society). Their participation in God's mission leads to transformation or healing in the world and through their agency they are able to contribute uniquely to that (build something tangible). All the way in the process, which is something ongoing and iterative over a lifetime, it is critical to be paying attention to what God is doing because it is God's mission they seek to join (prayerful discernment). This is an adventure of the imagination. It's not something formulaic that you can simply pull off the shelf or take from a how-to manual. It's an artful practice, as the best kind of cross-cultural mission has always been.

You in context

The students reflect on their sense of who they are, the gift they bring and how that gift might unfurl. That in itself can be challenging because it involves growing in self-awareness, facing their own struggles, and may well involve addressing internal scripts that undermine the gift. Spiritual direction, friendships, counselling, spiritual practices, retreats, can all contribute to this soulwork. We have found this particularly freeing for pioneers because the gift they bring is one that usually sees or imagines something different from business as usual. The Church can be a place that is suspicious of such seeing because it can seem threatening. But we create an environment in which we celebrate the gift of who students are, and say to them that we love the gift they bring. While it is helpful to reflect on pioneer ministry and what is meant by that, pioneering goes best when the pioneers stop aspiring to be some imagined other version of a pioneer and are able to become more fully the gift of themselves, trust their instincts, and imagine what might be possible as they act. That reflection on who you are is also one for teams and communities, not just individuals. So the 'you' can be plural. The stereotype of a pioneer is of a lone individual, the heroic leader, but this is an unhealthy picture. We have recently been inspired by friends in the Netherlands Protestantse Kerk, whose pioneer training is done for teams together, not just for solo leaders.

Training should be in situ or on the job. There is then a direct relationship between theory and practice. Questions arise from experience in the contexts that the students are in. The more live and real the context, the more effective the learning. The students are involved in mission practice while training. So the adventure of the imagination is not something to be embarked on down the line, once training is complete, but is participated in during training.

The turn to context is one of the most significant developments in the global conversation about theology.[3] It is a recognition that theology and the practice of mission and ministry are rooted in a particular time, space, geography, social location and culture. The conversation about contextual theology and contextual mission has largely arisen through global movements such as liberation theology in South America. However, it has grown as a theme in thinking about theology and mission in whatever local context a student is located.

There are various layers to context that are good for students to reflect upon. One is a societal level (see below). There are also more local geographical concerns such as what being Northern might mean with respect to faith in England. Context also relates to the local – a particular housing estate and the class and culture there. It may also relate to particular groups or networks of people – for example, young people who are struggling with mental health and anxiety, or steampunks.

It is really helpful in training to be exposed to examples of contextual theology and mission, both from other parts of the world and by visiting people who are doing it. This helps spark the imagination and get a feel for the sort of skills required. It also helps to create assessments for students, where they have to demonstrate theological reflection on their experiences of culture and context, including popular culture and the very local. It is also helpful for them to be exposed to creative articulations of spirituality and worship in the vernacular and to develop and create some for themselves in their own contexts. This involves play and an environment where experimentation is possible. In some theological colleges there is a focus on doing the liturgy right, and experimentation is not encouraged. And students should be helped with tools for mapping their contexts and produce work that shows they are able to use them in the multiple layers of their context.

Mission

Mission is a dynamic way of organizing training and theology. Rather than being a single module or one part of training, it is the lens through which all training for mission and ministry should be viewed and then organized and oriented. We have come to describe it as our True North. In other words, our hope and ambition is that all students who train with us will find their lives and ministry aligning with the pull towards God's mission, which is an overflow of love for the world and concern for its healing and redemption. The good news of Jesus Christ is shared for the sake of that world which God so loves. Learning about mission is learning about mission history, missiology and its attendant themes and frameworks, contextual and global theologies, questions of culture and context and the related attitudes and skills needed to move between those cultures. It is also to nurture a mission spirituality that fuels a life of mission, and to be steeped in the Bible's story of mission and especially the life of Jesus as pattern and example. And it is to be involved in and to reflect on one's own mission practice as well as to visit other contexts and learn from them. This is all such a rich repertoire to draw on in the adventure of the imagination.

There is a lovely book we use with students called *Theology Brewed in an African Pot*.[4] It's a local theology talking about God from within an African worldview, using imagery, parables and stories from that context. It's creative and insightful and wonderfully African. To be able to think, dream and talk about God in one's own language is so freeing. And it makes perfect sense. It's the logical fulfilment of Jesus saying to the disciples, 'As the Father sent me so I send you' (John 20.21). This was after the resurrection when he breathed on them and invited them to receive the Holy Spirit. He was sent into a local context and communicated with stories and signs and parables from that culture and now sends the disciples to do the same. When the Holy Spirit came on the day of Pentecost one of the results was that people heard in their own language. The history of mission is full of inspiring stories of translation into the vernacular in this way. It is often called inculturation or contextualization and we are fortunate to live at a time of awareness of these issues of mission and culture. History is also full of accounts of the imposition of Western theologies and culture so that, as missionaries shared the story of Jesus Christ, people got Western culture bundled with it and were expected to Westernize in order to become Christian. Their own cultural forms and approaches to spirituality and religion were often viewed with suspicion. Initially this new Western culture can seem exotic but the long-term problem is that Christianity just seems alien and the foreign-ness ends up being a huge barrier to faith. In many parts of the world unbundling is still taking place. This has been a big theme in the Anglican Church worldwide. Cathy did some research looking at the discussions at the Lambeth Conferences of Anglican bishops over one hundred years and found that this question of contextualization had been one of the central themes.[5] The Anglican Church has very much encouraged creative local theology and liturgy in response to these issues being raised.

This is not just a challenge for training people travelling to cultures in other parts of the world. The same issue is at play in our own contexts. The way that faith is framed in churches is foreign to many outsiders, so students need to be encouraged to find ways to do theology that relate to their communities, to work out what theology might look like when brewed in the pot of their community. This requires imagination and improvisation and ideally is something co-created together with the community, not just something the students do on their own. When the Holy Spirit comes, that community too should be able to hear in their own language. Training needs to enable this imaginative practice.

We have found books about art schools and the nurturing of behaviours for creatives very helpful when thinking how this might be done. For example, *The Creative Stance* summarizes seven behaviours that might help an artist to flourish.[6] They are imagination, provocation, risk, rigour, ambiguity, agency and resilience. It is very interesting to compare these with the kinds of behaviours expected for formation in theological colleges, which tend to be much more conforming and expecting of good behaviour.[7] It has led us to think that one of the most important roles for those of us designing training may be to reflect carefully on the air that students breathe in our training environments, and if necessary to change it. By 'those designing training' we are not just thinking of those involved in seminaries but also those in church leadership, and those running courses and leading small groups. Do members and students breathe air that encourages creativity, imaginative practice, hope and possibility, that connects with who they are and what they are called to? Or is the air concerned with right theology and right ways of doing church? Conformity and status quo?

It may seem bold to express this, but curiosity and exploration in this way are simply not encouraged in many churches and training institutions. We have observed that for students who train with us there is often a 'leaving home', or theological homelessness, that takes place as they go on this adventure, because it is such a different approach. They have really not been encouraged to do a lot of thinking for themselves or theological reflection. This can be unsettling for a time. But they do discover theology as a quest to think for themselves and the communities they are in, and they begin to find a new language that makes their world more coherent.

In *The Creative Stance* Grayson Perry introduces a section on rigour by describing two internal characters – hobbit and punk. Hobbit is the one who does the hard graft of learning the skill of making pots, glazes and learning the craft. He says that students will not be good artists without that learning, without putting in the 10,000 hours of work. But hobbit can be a bit boring so she also needs punk, who can come along and mess with things creatively, play, break pots, rework them, contravene conventions, take risks and so on. The interplay between these two characters leads to innovative practice. In theology, while here we are emphasizing context and imagination, the punk, the hobbitish rigour of engaging at depth with content is still important and, indeed, to be a good local theologian it helps to be versed in mission and theology from multiple contexts and cultures. So there is a rich array of material to work with, and for punk to draw on when brewing theology in the local pot. Clearly this is very different from the ways theology and ministry tend to be taught. In this approach, Western systematic theology, which is still the way much theology is framed in the West, becomes one local theology to understand and draw on alongside multiple others.

Church

The previous chapter was an attempt to reflect on church imaginatively and to paint a picture of church as a rich ecosystem full of possibilities, while also recognizing ways in which the Church gets stuck. For students in training, it is crucial that they engage broadly in these issues and develop thinking about mission and church. They are all located in particular traditions and denominations, with their own cultural sensibilities, theologies, sacred cows, understandings of ministry and how that is resourced, as well as various political environments.

These can be affected as much by the people in the structures as by the rubrics. So it is also important to reflect deeply on these particulars. The adventure of mission requires drawing on this rich tradition of possibility and navigating the current context faithfully and smartly. Yes, mission is an adventure but it does also require nous, as does any other adventure worth taking part in. It is essential that the navigating is done from a place of love for Christ, his Church and the world. We find that where students have been hurt by their experiences of church (which is fairly common), this needs processing so that they are able to act from a place of love rather than hurt. We like the notion of developing an undefended theology.

This depth of engagement and training will vary. For some their adventure of the imagination will mean that they are part of church congregations for a season but then will be planted out of the nursery once they have matured, connecting with the wider forest/ecosystem of church in multiple ways but freed up to put their energy into mission and building the kingdom in the world. They have not left church, they are still members of the body connected to Christ and one another.

For others that planting out may well be by way of the little congregations, small missional communities or Fresh Expressions of church that they start or engage with, whether in homes or the workplace. These smaller communities are great places to think Christianly about their call and adventure and to be supported in them and to engage with those outside the Church as they do so. Many of these communities are started and led by volunteers. Training for them needs to be accessible alongside working full time. A starting place might be to develop training in the four areas of reflection, service, worship and evangelism as outlined by Taylor, because those would make for a healthy local expression of church.[8]

For others, their life's call is to leadership in the Church whether as pioneers, laity or ordained ministers. For them building something tangible will include leading or starting a new community of disciples, a fresh expression of church, or one or more church congregations. For example, the expectation of an ordained pioneer minister in the Church of England is to start a new community of disciples. This is particularly the case where this is a salaried role. Within the wider eco-system of church it is also likely that there will be innovation and different funding models in mission that might resource building charities, community interest companies, social enterprises and so on. The Church should particularly reflect on how to resource pioneering and innovation at the edges, with fringe-dwellers as part of its mixed ecology.[9] There is a related set of understanding and skills required for those roles and the training for them will need more time and depth. We find it really helpful to see the ordained as a subset of the laity. Within the wider mission of God the ordained have a particular call, which among other things is to equip God's people for service in the world. This way of conceiving ministry might begin to help break the clerical paradigm.

Society

What is going on in the world and the country? What is happening with climate change, economics, politics, consumer culture, the postmodern turn or whatever term you prefer for the huge cultural shifts that are taking place?[10] How do we read it and make sense of it? What is happening with younger people? Where are the fringe-dwellers? John Taylor suggests that faith is looked at from inside the world, rather than looking at the world from inside the Church – so that should be the site of listening and awareness.[11]

Training needs to help students to engage positively with the world as a site of God's activity. At some basic level this means being present in the world so that we are on the same wavelength as others. John Taylor says, 'If the relevance of Jesus is really to be proclaimed in a world perspective his witnesses will have to look very much less "churchy". By which I mean they must not be organised as if they represented the interests of their own community and ideology.'[12] It involves looking for signs of the kingdom of God, or of the new creation.[13] Artists are close to the nerve endings of cultures, so paying attention to the arts and being able to reflect on them, whether in television, film, exhibitions, novels, songs, galleries, poetry and so on, is an important skill. There is a close relationship between art and prophecy. One of John Taylor's suggestions for training was to develop a 'school of prophets'.[14] By that he means those who can see and read the signs of the times, those who know what time it is. Depending on the student's tradition, they may need help and encouragement in not being judgemental of culture – some traditions are very good at seeing what is wrong with cultures and contexts rather than what is good. Every culture has both, but in terms of mission it is helpful to look first for the good and where God is at work. John Taylor's way of putting it is to say that 'sin is the last truth to be told'.[15]

Prayerful discernment

If mission is something that God is doing out of God's very being, then although there is lots of reflecting, thinking and theologizing to be done, it is also good to remember that this is a spiritual task. Training should help students to develop prayerful discernment. There are lots of great wells to draw from for this. With CMS pioneers we have drawn a lot from the contemplative practices of the Church, using things like *lectio divina*, the *examen*, spiritual direction, Ignatian spiritual exercises, silence and so on. I think the reason contemplative practices are so helpful is that they are about giving attention and awareness to God, to the world, and to yourself. So they enable us to notice what is going on, and encourage attentiveness. CMS works with churches over a three-year period to help them discern and join in with God's mission in their neighbourhood, and this process is founded on spiritual practices.[16] It can be creative rather than formulaic. What is important is to have a spirituality rooted in God's life and the Spirit.

Build something tangible

This is shorthand for saying that students should act for good in the world, joining in God's mission and his healing of creation as they witness to Christ. This can be done in multiple ways and should not just be reduced to a churchy agenda. For most students, this will be done in the midst of their life at work, at home, and in the community. For some it will be a role within the Church. A discussion on mission is developed later in the book (see Part Two).

Imagine training for Sarah and Joe

We recently hosted an international gathering, a *hui*, which was a space in which to reflect on training for mission practice.[17] One of the conversations was around how training can connect with the ordinary person in their context and enable them to lead. We came to describe these as the Sarahs and Joes, which came from stories that were shared. One 'Sarah' story was about someone on a housing estate with multiple issues of deprivation who was changed by coming to know and follow Jesus. She naturally gathered others together and shared with them, so that a fledgling Christian community grew up. She was clearly the best person to lead that community because she was a natural leader and she was indigenous, local rather than an outsider. In our experience at CMS mission generally goes best when it is locally led.[18] So some training could really help. But the Sarahs and Joes may well find that the sort of training available is simply not accessible to them, especially if they are from non-book cultures. This is to do both with the kind of training and the way it is framed and taught, which tends to suit particular learning styles. And it is also to do with not feeling at home in the culture of training. So there is a real need for imagination around appropriate training, which can be a great gift but does not necessarily need to be academic or traditional. At the *hui* we began to wonder how training could be created and navigated together with the Sarahs and Joes to reflect their concerns, context, language and frameworks. And we wondered whether learning could be imagined as a gift exchange in which Sarah and Joe and those leading the training all brought gifts to enable the learning. So, for example, the story of a pioneer in mission could be a gift shared to inspire learning. A question might be a gift to exploration. Joe might bring a gift from his community of something that holds an insight. A spiritual practice might be a gift.

One really good example of this was shared by Joe Hasler at the National Estate Churches Network. He was an ordained minister on a housing estate like that described above. He thought that the only way it would move forward was if the church found a Sarah or Joe to lead; they then discerned someone locally. They devised training as theological soup, where this 'Sarah' and others from the community came and discussed questions about theology, church, mission and ministry over soup together. This resonates with Clemens Sedmak's idea that theology is done by artisans and with the metaphor of the theologian as village cook – experimenting with locally available ingredients and always receptive to new cooks who arrive in the village.[19] The theological soup became a safe place, one within their culture, in which learning could take place and gifts were exchanged. This was all framed around the themes discussed in the book *Constants in Context*, which became a surprising gift.[20] It is a brilliant example.

However, below we suggest some of the ways in which training has got stuck and therefore does not help the Sarahs and Joes.

Becoming unstuck

Training and theological education has got stuck in a number of ways. It is a long way from the imagining above. We believe that there is a crisis of sorts and some radical change is required. As with the previous chapter we feel it is important to name some of the areas of stuckness.

1 It is overly academic. We are both huge fans of learning and see the value of rigour and study, so this is not an anti-academic comment. But for the vast majority the kind of learning that will help them is not going to be getting university degrees. When people are in ministry or in their workplace they will rarely be asked to write a 3,000 word essay.

Broadly speaking the categories of theology and the way it is organized in curricula in the theological colleges in the West have not changed much in the last 50 years and probably quite a lot longer.[21] This is really quite extraordinary. The world has changed so much in that time so as to be almost unrecognizable. As Gary Bouma puts it, 'Many institutions that train clergy still produce graduates suited to a society and culture that has now passed for more than quarter of a century.'[22]

2 A related issue is that the methods of teaching are also very Western and largely informed and shaped by the Enlightenment. Perry Shaw sums this up brilliantly:

There is increasing recognition that the traditional understanding of scholarship is educationally rigid and narrow. The perceived-as-normative approach to higher education reflects the preferred learning styles of only a small minority of the world's population – predominantly white Western males who approach learning through a rigid, linear, step-by-step empirical approach to reasoning.[23]

If the teaching is in the West you could argue that there is no problem in being Western, but at least frame the theology as a local theology, a particular take. Our experience at CMS is that a lot of students flourish with much more diverse teaching methods and creative approaches to assessment. For example, one student said that the theologies that helped him the most on his housing estate were African feminist theologies. The Western way of organizing tends to be siloed so training easily becomes fragmented rather than integrated. Paul Clark identifies four areas of fragmentation as between theory and practice; head, heart and hands; isolation from other disciplines; and sacred and secular.[24] What is required in context is usually integration in the midst of life. By way of contrast there are other disciplines where the approach to learning has changed considerably but it feels as though theology has been quite slow to catch up.

Add these things together and you can see that although the Church laments its lack of fringe-dwelling leaders in working-class cultures and ethnic minority groups and so on – what we have called the Sarahs and Joes above – it is hardly surprising![25] Indeed, it is probably inevitable with these forms of stuckness in training. It is hard enough for them to get recognized as leaders, because they don't fit the culture or expectations of those doing the selecting, and then it is even harder for them to flourish in training.

Church is dominated by the clergy – there is an unhealthy clericalism.[26] A recent government report named clericalism and tribalism as a problem in the wider culture of the Church that has contributed to abusive environments and needs changing.[27] Culture is sometimes described as 'the way we do things around here'. The way we do things around clergy has to do with the way ordination is described, where clergy are somehow seen as experts and treated as special, where they have a lot of power and control. The culture of the Church is such that in many places, if vocation is talked about, it is assumed that you are exploring being ordained. It is also very common that if you lead as a lay person, as Cathy and Jonny both do, the Church is forever asking whether you have thought of getting ordained, so you learn that is clearly more esteemed or valued, it is proper ministry.

With respect to training, the dominance is such that if you train to be ordained the Church will finance your training, whereas if you train to be a lay minister a local diocesan course is all that is usually available. And, to be honest, in the Church of England that is usually designed to train lay readers whose ministry is helping with leading church services – preaching, worship and pastoral care. So pioneers, for example, struggle to relate to it because it feels old-fashioned and churchy in focus. There is no resource available for their training, nothing more bespoke, even though they may well go on to plant and lead a fresh expression of church as an unpaid volunteer.

Church is often oddly and unnecessarily defensive. It can be defensive around theology, with the result that training becomes about ensuring that those trained have the right teaching, the right doctrine, are 'sound' and will be on-message when it comes to teaching about the atonement or sexuality or the sacraments or the Bible or whatever is perceived as under threat at the time. It can also be defensive about church practice – doing liturgy the right way, doing church right, dressing in particular ways. These two forms of defensiveness quickly lead to the Church being fearful and anxious, instead of being a great space in which to encourage innovative practice. These concerns are, of course, also all very churchy and introverted rather than focused on the real task of being in the world participating in God's mission.

3 This leads us to the final area of stuckness – mission is usually just one module in training. The environment we are now in surely requires a missional imagination and theology at the heart of training and those being trained to see themselves as leaders in mission. Our sense is that the sort of training we have developed and designed for pioneers at CMS, which is framed through a mission lens, would be a great way to frame training more broadly. On a positive note, in the Church of England those taking an academic award now do so in 'theology, mission and ministry'. So mission has at least made it into the language of the Church's training.

Innovation in training

One of our favourite of John Taylor's newsletters is on innovation in training, which he addresses to members of CMS in the name of 'Christ the Innovator'.[28] It seems so prescient in itself that we conclude this chapter with a summary of that letter and some quotations from it. The first section is entitled 'Academic ostriches', in which he explores the disconnect between the academy and the practice of mission on the ground. He calls for a training process that is context-centred rather than content-centred. He says that for too long we have insisted on cramming the minds of ordinands with the content of theology – the Bible, systematics, church history – and then applying this to various situational contexts. The truth of the Gospel is not that kind of truth. Rather, 'the proper aim of all theological training should be to help people to think biblically, to think theologically, to think Christianly'.[29]

The second section is headed 'On-the-job training'. *Mission Shaped Church* used that same phrase as a recommendation for the way pioneer ministers should be trained.[30] We designed the pioneer training at CMS on that basis, though we had not realized that Taylor had suggested it 50 years earlier! Context-based training has become much more widespread in the last few years.

In his third section, 'Disseminating the seminary', he tells the story of Ross and Gloria Kinsler, American missionaries in Guatemala, who developed the Theological Education by Extension movement in the late 1960s. They explained,

The fact: we were training the wrong people. We were preparing more and more young, unproven men for a middle-class ministry which was limited to five or ten churches, and ignoring the mature leaders who were doing the actual work of the ministry in churches ... The decision: we must take theological education to the natural leaders in the local congregations.

They took the risk of closing the residential seminary and setting up ten centres of dispersed learning. No fees or subsidies were given to any student apart from some limited transport expenses. In seven years, the number of students went from five to 200. The variety of approaches at the different centres served the differing needs and levels of the students.

Taylor sums up with a final section on pros and cons, contrasting between these two approaches in punchy fashion:

Traditional seminary training takes place before any experience; decentralized training combines academic work with practical experience. Traditional training is confined to the classroom lectures; decentralized training stimulates self-learning in the context of daily life. Traditional training limits candidates to the few who qualify on grounds of educational achievement, financial backing and age; decentralized training is much more widely available to students who qualify by virtue of leadership, perseverance and natural gifts. Traditional training takes people out of their milieu; decentralized training takes place where they live and work. Traditional training encourages a clerical, professional image of the ministry; decentralized training emphasizes a more functional servant role. Graduates of the old-style seminary feel that the Church owes them ordained status and a regular salary; the men and women trained by extension methods anticipate a tent-making ministry.[31]

We need to rise to the challenge of innovating appropriate training for our time and context, training that enables people to go on adventures of the imagination.

Exercising Creativity

Stay curious

Young children love asking 'Why?' This is a brilliant way to exercise imagination. In terms of creative thinking it is possibly the most important word you'll use.[32] Creative people are explorers who retain that childlike simplicity and urge to question everything. It will get you into trouble, of course, but keep asking the question. Add in a second question 'What if ...?' and it's amazing how creative you can be with just those two questions.

What holds these together is a posture of curiosity. If rule breaking is one key ingredient of creative thinking, then curiosity is another. Art schools know this. Research into London art colleges in *The Creative Stance* highlighted seven behaviours that make for a flourishing creative or artist as discussed above. But curiosity is the foundation: 'Curiosity is the substrate of creativity overlaid by an appetite for risk necessarily followed by determination.'[33] Will Gompertz says it is the tool that shapes artists' work as much as brush or chisel.[34]

It is an interesting question to ponder why children seem to lose some of their sense of wonder and curiosity as they get older. There is quite a contrast in that way between primary schools and secondary schools. Gordon Mackenzie, in his wonderful book *Orbiting the Giant Hairball*, describes taking classes in schools and finding that when he asked children which of them were artists, in the first grade all hands would go up, but the higher the grade the fewer hands went up.[35] Being playful and foolish and curious gets less rewarded the older you get, or so it seems. Teasing and cynicism are the enemies of curiosity. So as well as nurturing a space where curiosity is welcome, it may also need to be a space where certain negative behaviours or habits are resisted.

Exercises

When it comes to training and learning:

1 Ask why. It's as simple as that. Here are some of our whys to get you started:
   Why is training for church leading linked to academic university training?
   Why does the Church pay for the training of ordained clergy but not of lay leaders who will lead a church and perhaps not need to be paid?
   Why is training front-loaded and not spread out over a much longer period?

Why is being good rewarded in a way that curiosity is not?

Why do young children ask 'Why' a lot more than adults?

Why are our training colleges and courses more comfortable training hobbit than punk?

Why hasn't the way theology is taught changed much in the last 50 years?

Why do the Sarahs and Joes find it difficult?

Why is Western theology the default?

2   Ask 'What if'. See where it leads you. Here are some of our what ifs:

What if training for theology and mission and church leadership was more like art school?

What if thinking creatively was compulsory in the curriculum?

What if we focused more on learning than training?

What if training was for an adventure and you used the diagram above of the adventure of the imagination to explore and learn about mission?

What if you created a mission noticeboard that included the whole congregation on it?

What if training could fit around life and be more accessible with respect to work and family life?

What if all training was done through the lens of mission?

What if theology was taught as a process rather than a content?

What if Sarah and Joe were invited to design training for leaders?

What if it was assumed that training required practise on the job?

What if assessment was designed to demonstrate learning through practise and reflection on practise?

What if all those teaching were part time and involved part time in the practice they are teaching?

What if training required being immersed in other cultural settings?

What if training took Taylor's suggestion seriously – the proper aim of all theological training should be to help people to think biblically, to think theologically, to think Christianly?

What if apprenticeship was the main training model?

What if the norm assumed for ministry was tent making?

What if training was designed to help Jesus' witnesses look very much less churchy?

Notes

1 *CMS Newsletter*, No. 314, March 1968.

2 John Taylor, *The Primal Vision: Christian Presence amid African Religion* (London: SCM Press, 1963), p. 24.

3 Kevin Vanhoozer, 'One Rule to Rule Them All', in *Globalising Theology, Belief and Practice In An Era Of World Christianity* (Nottingham: Apollos/InterVarsity Press, 2007) p. 92; Stephen Bevans, *Models For Contextual Theology* (New York, NY: Orbis, 2002).

4 A. Orobator, *Theology Brewed in an African Pot* (New York: Orbis, 2008).

5 Cathy Ross, 'The Missiological Dimension of the Lambeth Conference', in Paul Avis and Benjamin Guyer (eds), *The Lambeth Conference, History, Theology and Purpose, The First 150 Years* (London: Bloomsbury/T&T Clark, 2018), pp. 297–315.

6 Bob and Roberta Smith, Edmund de Waal et al, *The Creative Stance* (London: Common Editions, 2016).

7 Jonny discusses this further in 'Prophetic Dialogue and Contemporary Culture', in Cathy Ross and Stephen Bevans (eds), *Mission on the Road to Emmaus* (London: SCM Press, 2015).

8 See the previous chapter.

9 John V. Taylor, *A Church Reshaped* (London: CMS, 1975), p. 10. Taylor commends the image of the Christian as a fringe-dweller.

10 In his Travel Diaries, USA and Mexico, 1963, p. 17. John Taylor

ardently believed that the world was facing a change 'more profound than the Renaissance of four hundred years ago'.

11 Travel Diaries, USA and Mexico, 1963, p. 19.

12 *CMS Newsletter*, No. 321, November 1968.

13 It is interesting that 'watch for the signs of God's new creation' is in the declaration for those being ordained as presbyter/priest in the Church of England, so it is already tied to ministry in that way.

14 *CMS Newsletter*, No. 295, July 1966.

15 John Taylor, *The Primal Vision: Christian Presence amid African Religion* (London: SCM Press, 1963), p. 172.

16 See churchmissionsociety.org/churches/partnership-missional-church/.

17 A *hui* is a Maori term for a gathering in a place that is flat, and a shared conversation.

18 This was recognized as far back in CMS's history as 1827, when a training institution was opened at Fourah Bay in Sierra Leone to train Africans for the ministry. This was the future University of Fourah Bay, where so many leading Sierra Leoneans were to study, though none perhaps more famous than the very first student, Samuel Crowther, later consecrated as the first African bishop of the Anglican Church.

19 Clemens Sedmak, *Doing Local Theology: A Guide for Artisans of a New Humanity* (Maryknoll, NY: Orbis, 2002), p. 20.

20 S. Bevans and R. Schroeder, *Constants in Context* (Maryknoll, NY: Orbis Books, 2004). See www.joehasler.co.uk; the paper on training is downloadable at www.joehasler.co.uk/wp-content/uploads/2014/05/5.Formation-of-a-local-person-for-olm-estate-priesthood.docx.

21 John Taylor was saying something very similar 50 years ago! For example, in *CMS Newsletter*, No. 339, June 1970, he suggested that there was an urgent need to rethink the curricula of training colleges all over the world so that what was studied actually bore some relevance to the world in which people lived.

22 Gary Bouma, *Australian Soul*, p. 105, quoted in Les Ball and Peter Boult, *Wondering About God Together* (Sydney: SCD Press, 2018), p. 10.

23 Perry Shaw and Havilah Dharamraj (eds), *Challenging Tradition: Innovation in Advanced Theological Education* (Cumbria: Langham Global Library, 2018), p. 43.

24 Paul Allan Clark, 'Pathways of Integration for Theological Knowledge: Integrative Knowing/Learning for Thesis Construction in Advanced Theological Studies', in Shaw and Dharamraj, *Challenging Tradition*, p. 191.

25 In *CMS Newsletter*, No. 314, March 1968, Taylor says about the

forms of training: 'In the West these are too middle-class and evoke no response from industrial man.'

26 In *Travel Diaries, USA and Mexico*, 1963, p. 19, John Taylor reflected on the need for the death of clericalism.

27 See www.iicsa.org.uk/publications/investigation/anglican-chich ester-peter-ball (accessed 15.8.2019).

28 *CMS Newsletter*, No. 377, January 1974.

29 *CMS Newsletter*, No. 377.

30 Graham Cray (ed.), *Mission Shaped Church* (London: Church House Publishing, 2004), p. 148.

31 *CMS Newsletter*, No. 377.

32 John Hegarty, *Hegarty On Creativity: There Are No Rules* (London: Thames & Hudson, 2014), p. 52.

33 Hegarty, *Hegarty*, p. 64.

34 Will Gompertz, *Think Like an Artist* (London: Penguin Random House, 2015), p. 62.

35 Gordon Mackenzie, *Orbiting the Giant Hairball* (New York: Viking Penguin, 1998), chapter 1.

PART TWO

Mission

3

An Adventure of the Imagination

The concept of mission has certainly gained currency in recent years. Definitions of mission abound, with the Five Marks of Mission and its various iterations being particularly popular.[1] Some say if mission is everything, then nothing is mission, or what then is especially distinctive about mission? These are fair questions and we have found mission a challenging concept to pin down exactly because it is so all-encompassing and is about the whole of life and God's kingdom. The Five Marks are neither a perfect nor a complete definition of mission. They do not say everything we might want to say about mission in today's world but they do form a good working basis for a holistic approach to mission. Mission is a longing see all things renewed – our relationships with God and with one another, with our environment and species, with our societies – our world and our cosmos. It is the healing and redemption of all things under the Lordship of Christ. This chapter offers some of John Taylor's particular insights on mission. We start with evangelism, within the context of holistic mission, as that was an early emphasis of Taylor's and is foundational for CMS.

CMS's founding story is to share Jesus with those who do not know him in places where the Gospel is not known. This is what mission was about for our early CMS forebears and it is still a distinctive mark of CMS today – sharing the good news of Jesus with those who are beyond the reach of the Church. This means engaging in evangelism – a kind of evangelism that uplifts and shows forth Jesus Christ so that, as John Taylor wrote in one of his CMS newsletters, people may see him, 'and truly seeing, may believe in him whose coming has completely transformed the human situation and through whom a totally new life is available'.[2]

John Taylor was well aware that the practice of evangelism could be much abused, so he offered five aspects that should never be missing from its practice.

1 Evangelism is witness. Witness must take place within the context of a human relationship. True witness implies a concern both for the Gospel and for the other person, otherwise this becomes merely a conversation or an uncaring encounter with the other person.

2 Evangelism is people. Taylor insists that the Gospel must advance from person to person. This requires sustained, long-term relationships and can be costly. Ever since Jesus stated that he is the truth, this means that truth is personal rather than propositional. Spiritual truth is something 'we *meet* – or rather, something that meets us'.[3] In a lovely metaphor, Taylor likens it to love for one's partner: 'It comes home to me in the same sort of way as the truth about my wife and our love for each other comes home to me. I know it, but personally and by encounter.'[4] Evangelism is a relational activity.

3 Evangelism is service. Caring for people leads Gospel bearers into a ministry of compassion. Reflecting on Paul's words in 2 Corinthians 4.5: 'For we do not proclaim ourselves; we proclaim Jesus Christ as Lord and ourselves as your slaves for Jesus' sake.' Taylor expands on service as 'the Service of human need, the Service of human significance (noticing people) and the Service of reconciliation'.[5] Evangelism is more than proclamation only and involves a servant witness. Whether mission is fulfilled mainly in service or in evangelism is a false dichotomy. Service is a demonstration of Christian love, but if it is done in order to prove something then, according to Taylor, it proves nothing.

4 Evangelism is worship. Taylor roots this in a sacramental understanding of worship. He writes that 'a true act of Christian worship at one and the same time makes manifest the Gospel and recalls its witnesses to the heart of the mat-

ter'.[6] As people come to know Christ, they long to worship because 'the Lord wins men's [sic] hearts long before he wins their logic'.[7]

5 Evangelism is prayer. Taylor asserts that nine-tenths of evangelism may well depend on prayer, and that is the responsibility of all of us.

Imagine mission as sharing the Gospel in all humility and gentleness

Evangelism must be practised with all humility and gentleness. In a newsletter reflecting on Christian witness in China, Taylor sharply criticized the use of power and wealth in evangelism:

> The use of superior power to commend the Gospel, whether the power of money, or the power of expertise or the power of access to political authority, even though it is used to do good and to serve the needy unconditionally, may result in conversions, but many of them will be conversions to the more successful way of life, not conversions to Jesus Christ.[8]

He believed that when the reaction to this approach sets in it may also mean a rejection of Jesus, whose name is associated with this method. He makes a plea that we 'power-conscious Westerners' should learn the secret of Paul's method, 'For I decided to know nothing among you except Jesus Christ, and him crucified. And I came to you in weakness and in fear and in much trembling' (1 Cor. 2.2–3). Taylor implored us to open our minds and to see things from the Chinese point of view in order to prepare ourselves for a creative interchange with Chinese people when the opportunity presents itself. He reminds us that, at that time (1973), 'our most telling form of witness to our Lord's power will not be the things we can say to China but our readiness to listen to what China is saying to us'.[9] This remains a continuing challenge in each of our contexts, because we need to listen to what each of them is saying to us and what gifts they may bring to us.

In our Western contexts, as with the early Church, it may be that our evangelism is best modelled and communicated by lifestyle and presence. In a newsletter where he reflected on the challenges Christians face as a minority in Muslim countries and in the Middle East, Taylor quoted Kenneth Cragg, who reminds us of the approach of the minority early Church:

> it was not by any despairing withdrawal from city and market that they conquered the world; not by any proud isolation or selfish security; not by any impatient violence but by the winning influence of a gracious faith, they mastered the family, the school, the empire.[10]

An evangelism of presence and a lifestyle of hope and perseverance can be an attractive witness. This approach to mission may be most fruitful when engaged in by a team or a community who are discovering together what it means to live out the practical implications of their discipleship in each new context.

Imagine mission as sharing the Gospel with creativity and imagination

We need a fresh approach to the presentation of the Gospel and a new approach to evangelism because the Christendom era is over and people no longer, 'know what it [faith] was nor find meaning in it when it is explained'.[11] In his book *The Act of Creation*, Arthur Koestler suggested that creativity derives from two normally incompatible ideas and he affirms the vitality and power of signs, symbols and analogies. He also emphasized the value of seeing the connections, and Taylor writes that this 'reminds me that a great part of true evangelism is just that – an ability to see the connection between the changeless Gospel and the immediate circumstance'.[12] He believes that because so few have or learn this ability, 'the Gospel lives only in its own, expected frame of reference and there is no creative, fresh vitality in its presentation'.[13] We love the idea of mission as an 'adventure of the imagination' – a phrase that Taylor uses in his book *The Primal Vision*.[14] In that book he is reflecting on the question of translation in relation to primal religions in Africa. We desperately need the gift of imagination and in our postmodern and post-Christian Western contexts an indirect method of evangelism is more likely to gain a hearing and response. He argues for more creativity, more imagination and more gentle and nuanced 'cultivation' as we engage with people,

> The evangelist, as Paul well knew, has to cultivate what grows from God's planting without trampling it with his own dogmatic boots ... And may it not be that if we are ever to learn how to sing the Lord's song in the strange land of our secular world we shall have to learn to use more of his obliquity?[15]

If we do not use the divine imagination given to us, we will be embarrassed by a world capable of far more imagination than the Church itself. What we need is not more technique but more imagination, '"to see the unseen" in what is familiar and contemporary and to offer it to men [sic] as a parable, in all its liability to be missed or misunderstood'.[16] We need to cultivate our imaginations along these lines so that we can intrigue and surprise when we present the Gospel and give people the opportunity to discover for themselves what the cost of discipleship means and what gifts Jesus brings.

Imagine mission as local

Mission is best done by the insiders or the local people. The Gospel is universal but the Gospel's thought forms, metaphors and the way it is communicated will vary from place to place and age to age. Each age and context needs imagination to communicate the Gospel afresh. This is best done by insiders. If the Gospel is to be genuinely understood and lived out by a local culture and context, then the locals are the best ones to work this out.

We need to be far more radical in allowing this to happen.

We – whoever 'we' may be – the Westerners, the older Christians, the incomers onto a local housing estate – need to let go and allow the insiders to get hold of the Gospel, understand it and live it in ways that make sense to them. Too often we want to protect, guard and defend the Gospel, thereby limiting its power and potential to embed and root itself in the local context.

We become, in Taylor's phrase, 'the guardians of universality'[17] and therefore mistrust the local and the particular. We need not be afraid of the local; instead we need to allow the locals to mine their own culture for its riches, seams and veins that can begin to communicate the Gospel afresh. The Word is basic everywhere, but 'the thought forms, the metaphors, the logic in which it is communicated, these differ from culture to culture and from age to age'.[18] Even the story of salvation may have to be told differently, as each of the four gospels demonstrates. Worship, theology, ethics, ministry – each of these must be universal but must be rooted in the local context if they are to be authentic and make sense in a particular context.

Let's look at two striking examples from John Taylor to illustrate this. The first is from Pakistan in 1969 and picks up the idea of how best to communicate the Gospel by using signs and symbols. At this stage Pakistan had been independent for only 20 years and was (and still is) a largely Muslim country. Taylor questioned whether the public display of the cross was the most appropriate way of representing the Gospel in that context. This was not because he wanted to mute or silence the Gospel but because he believed that what this sign communicated in that context was anything but the Gospel for Pakistan. As a symbol it encapsulated centuries of misunderstanding, and reminded people not only of the Crusades but also of more recent Christian–Muslim violence. He ultimately agreed that the cross is too unique and fundamental a symbol to be given up, but it all depends on how it is displayed. He cited the example of a Christian hospital in the Punjab that created an uproar with their display of a floodlit cross on the top of their building. 'That, I would contend, is the wrong way to honour the symbol of the Crucified.'[19]

He then pondered on what might be a more appropriate symbol of service and sacrifice for Pakistan. He found it in a humble, domestic object already present in many Christian homes – the short-handled broom that looks like a sheaf of straw. 'If it were adopted as the mark of Christian allegiance it would certainly be a scandal and an object of shame, just as the gallows-cross was in the early days of the Church.'[20] He explained that the term 'Christian' was almost synonymous with 'sweeper' because 45 per cent of Christians in (then) West Pakistan were indeed sweepers. Another 35 per cent belonged to an even poorer section of society, the landless serfs. This was a poor church, a struggling church trying to live out its faith in a majority Muslim context. Here is an example that demonstrates the kind of imagination and creativity we need in order to contextualize the Gospel locally, using local symbols that are immediately understood within that context. We believe that this is the kind of radical thinking and questioning that we need to engage in today in order to communicate the Gospel afresh.

Another example is from India, where Metropolitan Lakdasa de Mel[21] challenged the local church to 'take off the trousers before we can put on the dhoti'.[22] He implored the Indian Church to 'put off her institutionalism, for it is that which is western through and through'.[23] We can see that this approach is dishonouring to Christ if Jesus Christ is only presented in a foreign way, for how will Indians come to know him as one of them, living in their neighbourhoods, if he is presented only in trousers, rather than in local clothing? The Gospel must permeate all of Indian society so that Indians can live and experience the Gospel in an Indian way. This also applies to language and translation – both the linguistic translation of Christian concepts but also translating these into an authentically Indian expression of what it means to live as Indian Christians in their place and space. Where might the Spirit be at work to help them discern that? A clue might be in their great Hindu heritage. Could Indian Christians mine their rich heritage of artists, musicians, thinkers, philosophers and poets so that the Gospel can be presented and experienced as a truly Indian treasure?

If so, this opens up all sorts of interesting and exciting possibilities. Scottish mission historian Andrew Walls has alerted us to the emergence of world Christianity and the global Church. He warns us in the West against arrogance and myopia:

> Like the old Jerusalem Christians, Western Christians have long grown used to the idea that they were guardians of a 'standard' Christianity; also like them, they find themselves in the presence of new expressions of Christianity, and new Christian lifestyles ... to display Christ under the conditions of African, Indian, Chinese, Korean and Latin American life.[24]

We can react by wanting to protect our own version of Christianity and declare it as the normative one, the default setting. Or we can declare that each expression is indeed valid and then proceed to enjoy our own in isolation from the others. Walls introduces the temple and body metaphors from Ephesians and declares that, 'The Ephesian metaphors of the temple and of the body show each of the culture-specific segments as necessary to the body but incomplete in itself.'[25] We need one another in order to enlarge, correct, challenge and refocus our own understanding of Christ. Then these different worlds and fresh ideas can be just as useful to Christianity worldwide as Greek philosophy and thought have been to Europe.

Even more exciting is that this uncovering of the Gospel is a two-way process of mutuality. Christianity is nurtured by and in cultural encounters and then in turn develops and nurtures those cultures. For example, it was only when the Chinese took in Jesus and nurtured and understood him in Confucian ways that he became Chinese enough to be understood. In this way other cultures can also benefit from the 'Chinese-ness' of the Gospel and the creative interchange that this sparks. The local church must be allowed and permitted to develop and express its Christian life and faith in ways pertinent and relevant to its own context.

This is as true in Britain as it is overseas: 'I mean the house church in Britain, the outlying bush church in Africa, and any other local Christian community group.'[26] These are the growing edges of the Church but the centre finds it hard to allow these edges to grow. 'The guardians of universality mistrust the particular, and thereby destroy the source from which a greater universality might arise.'[27] Taylor does not have a romanticized view of this, nor is he sentimental about it. He is well aware that nationalism and ethnocentrism could arise and cut off the local church from the wider Christian body. But the opposite can also be true. The world-wide Church is renewed by insights from the local and the particular – insights that offer a wider perspective to the whole. Authentic universality is neither maintained nor created by control from the centre. This mistrust from the centre is ironic because it is exactly when we allow our indigenous values and virtues, redeemed by Christ, to be offered to and experienced by the wider Church that a 'greater universality' can then develop in the world Church.

It is also important not to be backward looking in the attempt to be indigenous. We need a forward-looking faith that has an eye to the future. Sometimes we can revert back to old ways, believing this to be local or indigenous when it is just nostalgia and wistful longing for the past. Taylor believes that a Christian perspective is to experience the present 'flowing towards them, new, out of the future'.[28] Jesus' resurrection broke into time and rearranged time for evermore so that we do not have to be beholden to the tyranny of past events. This is both hopeful and challenging – to be able to discern the work of the Spirit in the coming of the new. Mission and renewal will 'stir the Church into continual discontent with even the best of its traditional forms. It is sent into a world of change and progression, and it must get on with it. But that means different things in different places.'[29]

How do we ensure that the local does not disintegrate into syncretism? Perhaps we worry too much about this. It is always easier to spot syncretism in someone else's culture and context than in our own! We need to trust in the power of the Spirit to guide and lead each local church and trust them to be able to differentiate between local cultural appropriation and inappropriate syncretism. As Taylor asserts, '*To be indigenous, therefore, means simply to be free to respond to Christ and to the world without any of the self-consciousness which is imposed by the attitudes of others.*'[30]

Imagine mission as prophetic

Mission needs to discern the signs of the times and be alert to the winds of the Spirit. In other words, it needs to be prophetic. This is what Taylor calls an 'inspired opportunism'.[31] In his final newsletter as General Secretary he offers three concepts as a way to explore what it takes to become a prophet. These are sight, sign and solidarity.

Taylor's first concept is that prophecy begins with the eye that sees. He reminds us that one Old Testament word for prophet is *roeh* – literally one who sees, a see-er. However, he believes that it is even more important to see ordinary things in an extraordinary way. The prophetic impulse begins with the seeing eye. 'Something confronts us with the strong sense that it bears a hidden meaning. If we look and wait its significance will break through.'[32] He cites biblical examples of the woman stirring yeast into dough, or fishermen dragging their nets full of fish onto the beach, or a cage of sparrows at the market. Jesus is able to see all these ordinary images as something more – metaphors of God's kingdom and discipleship. He sees them as communicating the kingdom of God and God's love. The gift of seeing the ordinary in an extraordinary way is needed as we engage in mission today.

Sign is Taylor's second concept. He believes that our minds have become blunted by a computer age and that we need to retrain ourselves to communicate in signs and symbols. We need to learn this from childhood. 'We must learn, and help our children to grow up learning, how to say it with flowers, or with a picture card or gift deliberately chosen because it can convey a message to the one to whom it is given and to no one else.'[33] This is a beautiful picture of developing our imaginations from an early age. The Old Testament prophets did this effectively. Prophets such as Isaiah, Jeremiah and Hosea spent much of their ministry in symbolic acts and living symbolic lives. Jesus, of course, was the supreme giver of signs and always ready to be a sign himself. The washing of his disciples' feet, the sharing of bread and wine, the wedding at Cana, his healing miracles are all important signs and symbols of his own mission. We need to recapture this ability to be signs of the kingdom of God in ways that communicate and pique interest, rather than spell out the meaning in a literal, dreary or dogmatic way.

Taylor's third and most challenging concept is solidarity. For 'in order to be a sign of the Gospel we have to walk the sacrificial way of solidarity with the people and the situation concerning which we have been given a gift of insight and a word to proclaim'.[34] This is a hard calling and he cites the prophets Jeremiah and Ezekiel as examples of men who embodied this. Ezekiel was instructed by the Spirit of God 'to enact the ultimate sign of solidarity' with Israel: 'Then lie on your left side, and place the punishment of the house of Israel upon it; you shall bear their punishment for the number of the days that you lie there' (Ezek. 4.4). Taylor postulates that the writer of the last Servant Song in Isaiah 53 might have had Jeremiah or Ezekiel in mind as he composed it, although by the end of the song this idea has been overtaken by a greater figure that can only be fulfilled by Jesus. Solidarity may be the hardest and most challenging aspect of mission.

Imagine mission as costing everything

Mission will mean conversion and conversion is a turning, a radical reorientation of a person towards God, a changed relationship through repentance and faith in Christ. We need to face some difficult questions about what conversion means and how it works in cultures with little or no Christian heritage, and to be realistic about the challenge this presents. 'But is that kind of repentance and faith immediately possible to a man [sic] whose ideas and attitudes are completely untouched by what we might call the presuppositions of the Bible?'[35] Words such as 'sin, life, and death' may mean something different or even nothing at all, so something else must happen before the Gospel can even be heard. The culmination of evangelism is conversion, but it seems that God may be more patient with people than we are, and that God's ways of eliciting a response are more varied and unexpected than any of ours.

Although God may be patient, it is nonetheless true that conversion may cost us everything and can cause much suffering. During Taylor's visit to Nepal in 1968 he met with Christians who had been imprisoned for their faith. He spent time with Prem, a Nepali pastor who had spent four years in prison for his faith in Christ. Although he knew that baptism could result in imprisonment, he continued to baptize people and had baptized 23 people in the previous two years. 'But, he said, I never baptize anyone until I know that he or she is able to bear suffering. For me, that was the most significant word of the evening.'[36] Taylor experienced more of the same in Moscow, later on the same trip. He met with an Orthodox priest who had suffered much. His number of baptisms had doubled each year in the last three years. Most of the converts were students who found no hope for their existential angst in Marxism. They asked, 'What can save the inner springs of humanity in a human being? And what do they derive from in the first place?'[37] In that context, conversion almost certainly meant the ruin of a good career and a possible reporting of the church to the authorities. It is a salutary reminder that conversion to Christ costs not less than everything.

Non-essential obstacles must be removed, but we cannot remove the cross. 'And that, in its specific form for each situation, confronts the would-be disciple at the start, it isn't reserved for more mature Christians.'[38] The rich young ruler had to abandon his privilege as a condition of discipleship and his coming to Christ had social as well as spiritual implications. There are no universal rules – each situation has to be measured and judged afresh. 'So the heart of the problem seems to be to distinguish between the stone of stumbling Christ lays before those who approach him as an inescapable demand, and the stumbling blocks which we create unnecessarily while calling them basic.'[39] This requires much discernment and wisdom and is a harder road to follow.

Taylor was firm that we need, 'to recover our nerve about the supernatural'.[40] He was particularly concerned that young people had 'written off the church and found Christianity wanting'.[41] He believed that they were searching for a cause to which they could dedicate their lives and they had scorned Christianity. He encouraged a renewed belief in the supernatural, a recovery of meditation that introduces 'mystery and miracle' into their lives and a development of Christian 'communes' or communities. Only in this way could the Church regain any credibility among young people looking to make a difference in the world. 'I envisage these Christian communes of "tribes" fashioning a style of living which will express and intensify, in very great freedom, the full ambiguity of the human person – his total solitariness and his total corporateness, his mystical capacities and his passion for justice.'[42] We have seen elements of this in the rise of New Monasticism and in missional communities today for those who are wanting to live out their faith in ways that combine both a renewal of spirituality and a commitment to community engagement.

This then leads to a salvation which is 'down-to-earth', because salvation is far from an abstract concept. Jesus only knows saving faith in concrete responses. Salvation comes to Zacchaeus when his new relationship with Jesus compels him to return half his goods to the poor and repay four times what he has cheated. Salvation comes to the Samaritan leper, not when he is healed, but when he returns to thank Jesus. Furthermore, no one is saved by acknowledging a doctrine. Taylor writes:

> You will search in vain for any systematic doctrine of salvation in the incidents in which he makes men [sic] whole. In his vocabulary no distinction is made between the healing of a body and the saving of a soul, and in his eyes faith is equally faith whether it be the instinct of a foreign army officer to take him at his word or the commitment which he prays that Peter will not lose in his hour of temptation.[43]

For Taylor there are five biblical elements in almost every salvation event: judgement, intervention, victorious rescue, spacious freedom, and mission.

Imagine mission as dangerous

Our practice of mission is undergirded by our theology. What if our theology is not safe? Taylor believes that there is no such thing as a safe theology, because a theology that is in touch with the world will be a living theology with all its attendant risks, mistakes and developments. Theology has a missionary role in its task to communicate the truths of the Gospel to a world that is constantly changing. Therefore theology must emerge out of a dynamic encounter with the world. A theology of mission that is grounded and rooted in current realities must be interdisciplinary and ask searching and challenging questions. In 1976 Kenyan theologian John Mbiti asserted that we are kerygmatically universal but theologically provincial.[44] In other words, we believe in and proclaim the Gospel but we allow our theology to remain limited and constrained by our own safe, provincial horizons.

On visits to India, Taylor encountered a distinctive Indian theology which had emerged from the creative response of Hindu thinkers to Jesus. He dared to suggest that this 'has brought about a kind of renaissance within Hinduism itself'.[45] He devoted an entire newsletter to Indian theology that had emerged in conversation with Hinduism, lamenting the fact that European and American theological schools had taken little notice of it. He finds this to be 'absurd' because this theology offers us a new approach to the meaning of Christ. He insisted on the 'Christwardness of Hinduism' and explored how some deeply Hindu ideas can be helpful in opening up our appreciation of Jesus. Taylor does not accept everything uncritically, but what is exciting is his openness to new thought forms, to different worlds and fresh ideas, so that, 'Indian thought can be made just as useful to Christianity as Greek thought has been to Europe'.[46]

He did the same in his encounter with Japanese theologian Kosuke Koyama, picking up on Koyama's insight of 'the crucified mind'. Taylor gets to the heart of the issue here with this extraordinary insight: 'Only the crucified mind is free and self-emptied enough to enter a people's context and culture and feel the pressures of its particular need and pain.'[47] He continues that 'what the whole human family is waiting for is the emergence of a crucified African mind, a crucified Chinese mind, a crucified European mind'.[48] These are the kinds of insights that emerge from very different local contexts and demonstrate what the local can offer to the Church universal in terms of theology, witness, discipleship and spirituality. Taylor does the same with his reading of African theologians, championing the contributions they can offer to our understanding of theology. He was particularly taken by Mbiti's discussion of Bantu approaches to time and the contrast with the Western post-Renaissance emphasis on progress and continual change. He asserted that much more dialogue was needed between these two understandings of time, and encouraged a greater openness to learning from other contexts and worldviews.

In order to communicate theological insights more effectively, metaphor and symbol may again help us with how we can speak of God. 'Metaphor is all we have to help us express our understanding of God', and Taylor emphasized again the importance of symbol and image. 'The symbols and images we use will go on being effective as long as they are drawn from experiences which are not wholly remote from us.'[49] A good example of this emerged from his visit to Ceylon in 1969. The Church there had to cease to be foreign. How does this happen in a context where Christians are a tiny minority? Is it selling out and compromise to offer flowers and incense as part of Christian devotion, for example? Must Christians insist on Sunday as a day of rest when society observes a different day? Questions and issues of this type must face Christians everywhere if we are to be relevant and faithful.

Another powerful and dangerous story was of a young Anglican monk in an ashram that he shared with his Buddhist friends. On the walls of the chapel are a work by Rodin, the

figure of Shiva, and the gentle calm of the Buddha in meditation. Nearer the front of the chapel are Michelangelo's Moses
and another Old Testament character, and pictures of the
Christ. Taylor ponders, 'Is this truth or compromise? And is
this Christian priest right to include in the preparatory part of
his Communion Service a reading from the Buddhist texts?'[50]

Such are the hard questions that face us there and everywhere as we struggle to communicate the Gospel in context.
Just as Jacob wrestled with an angel, so we too need to wrestle
with theological questions and issues that arise as we engage
in mission. It is a serious undertaking. It is a long undertaking
with no certain outcome. We need to experiment. We will make
mistakes, but it is absolutely necessary if we are to develop a
missional theology that is fit for purpose and be of service to
the world and the Church. 'All theology which is earnest is also
dangerous. It is an act of adoration fraught with the risk of
blasphemy.'[51] This is why mission can be dangerous.

Imagine mission as joining in with God

Perhaps John Taylor is best known these days for his succinct
and popular summary of mission as 'seeing what God is doing
in a situation and trying to do it with him'.[52] He rooted this
in Christology and the Spirit, for Jesus had his eyes opened by
the Spirit to recognize God at work in the world: 'Jesus said
to them, Very truly, I tell you, the Son can do nothing on his
own, but only what he sees the Father doing; for whatever the
Father does, the Son does likewise' (John 5.19). As disciples,
we are called to take the same position in relation to Jesus as
Jesus had in relation to his Father. Mission means joining in
the unfinished task of creation and redemption. It is better to
start with our theology more inclusive rather than too narrow.

When did Jesus start his mission? The first active verbs used of
Jesus are when he was in the temple debating with the teachers.
We are told that he was 'listening' and 'asking them questions'.
So listening and asking questions are a vital part of engaging in
mission and of our theological reflection on mission.

Mission also involves proclamation of the Gospel, witness and service, 'what we tell, what we are and what we do'.[53] If any of those three strands is missing, then our mission could become distorted or truncated.

Mission is about sharing the Gospel – always aware of the context and of possibilities for newness and change. It is about listening to and learning from those contexts so that we too are changed and transformed as we receive the gifts of the other. It is about living and presenting the Gospel imaginatively so that people can be intrigued and explore for themselves, with the inspiration of the Spirit, what it looks like to be followers of Jesus in their context. It is about letting the local flourish so that mission and discipleship are rooted in the local context. Then the universal will also flourish as local insights enrich the Church everywhere. It is about conversion and the cross. It is about a crucified mind. It will cost us everything. It is about the gift of sight and the challenge of solidarity. It is about living with a theology that is in touch with the world, that is experimental, that is willing to take risks. It is about being willing to theologize and to live dangerously.

Imagine mission as trying to make the world a better place. Imagine if mission were as simple – and as complex – as that. Essentially mission is the redemption and healing of all things under Christ. It is a yearning to see all things renewed – our relationships, our societies, our environment, our world and our cosmos. 'Mission means joining him, as he joins the Father, in the unfinished task of creation, redemption and perfection of the whole universe.'[54]

Exercising Creativity

Combinatory play

One of the stories used in lots of books on creative thinking is the design of the Gutenberg printing press.[55] Johannes Gutenberg noticed the way that a screw press was used to press grapes in winemaking and he borrowed the idea from that field and used it to solve a problem in another – printing. The new technology of the printing press changed the world. A similar story is told of James Dyson noticing the extraction of dust at an industrial factory and combining that with a vacuum cleaner to invent the Dyson.

Placing two things together that wouldn't normally be side by side is a very simple but powerful idea we touched on above with Koestler. It's also something that we can all do. Einstein called it combinatory play.[56] Usually that creativity comes by connecting two ideas from two different areas. It is important to be an explorer and get outside your area.[57]

In relation to mission, the essence of contextual mission is exactly that – placing the Gospel alongside local culture and seeing where connections are. Jesus told a very simple parable saying that the kingdom of God is like a teacher who took something old and something new out of the cupboard (Matt. 13.52). He too knew this art of combinatory play. Here are a couple of examples from pioneers who have trained with us at CMS. David connected with lads who were keen on boxing and he combined a fresh expression of church with boxing. He developed a wonderful prayer experience combining Compline with a boxing ring where there were prayer stations in each corner of the ring and every couple of minutes a bell would ring to move to the next one. His question was 'How do you do church for people who like to punch stuff?' A creative and unlikely combination! Or pioneers working with spiritual seekers have taken something old, *lectio divina*, a contemplative way of reading the Bible, and combined it with card reading using the Jesus deck, a pack of cards with suits of the four Gospels and a scripture on each card. In a culture used to card reading this makes perfect sense of reading the Bible. Another creative and unlikely combination. It doesn't always have to be something strange. Using what is in front of you can also be helpful. Jesus' parables and metaphors were of everyday things.

Exercises

1 Wander your neighbourhood, or reflect on a group of people or network that you are part of, or a local culture, and notice the signs and symbols that are part of their world. Choose one. Is there a Gospel story or something in the tradition that you are drawn to in relation to that? Combine the two – where does that lead you?

2 Taylor says that metaphor is all we have to help us express our understanding of God. Find a new metaphor to explore in relation to God. Or write a parable of the kingdom that begins 'The kingdom of God is like ...'

3 Robert Poynton suggests a threefold practice for improvisation: notice more, let go, and use everything.[58] This is so simple and yet it leads to the kind of combining that makes great connections. Try it as a practice in your locale. Pay attention. What do you see? What do you notice? What might you need to let go of in your own thinking or expectations? What is in your hand that you could use?

4 Street Wisdom is a practice of wandering a neighbourhood and noticing things that have a street wisdom to make connections with a question you are asking and to take with you. Organize a group street wisdom activity – see www.streetwisdom.org.

Notes

1 The Five Marks of Mission are: 1. To proclaim the Good News of the kingdom. 2. To teach, baptise and nurture new believers. 3. To respond to human need by loving service. 4. To transform unjust structures of society, to challenge violence of every kind and pursue peace and reconciliation. 5. To strive to safeguard the integrity of creation, and sustain and renew the life of the earth. www.anglicancommunion.org/mission/marks-of-mission.aspx (accessed 15.1.2020).

2 *CMS Newsletter*, No. 270, April 1964.

3 *CMS Newsletter*, No. 307, September 1967.

4 *CMS Newsletter*, No. 307.

5 Travel Diaries, Australasia, 1966, p. 49.

6 *CMS Newsletter*, No. 270, April 1964.

7 Travel Diaries, Pakistan, Nepal, Afghanistan, Moscow, 1968, p. 36.

8 *CMS Newsletter*, No. 369, March 1973.

9 *CMS Newsletter*, No. 369.

10 *CMS Newsletter*, No. 275, October 1964.

11 *CMS Newsletter*, No. 295. July 1966.

12 Travel Diaries, Malaya, Hong Kong, Japan, New York, 1965, p. 3. See Arthur Koestler, *The Act of Creation* (London: Hutchinson & Co, 1964).

13 Travel Diaries, Malaya, Hong Kong, Japan, New York.

14 John Taylor, *The Primal Vision* (London: SCM Press, 1963), p. 41.

15 *CMS Newsletter*, No. 295, July 1966.

16 *CMS Newsletter*, No. 295.

17 *CMS Newsletter*, No. 299, December 1966.

18 *CMS Newsletter*, No. 299.

19 *CMS Newsletter*, No. 323, January 1969.

20 *CMS Newsletter*, No. 323.

21 He was the last Metropolitan Bishop of India, Pakistan, Burma and Ceylon.

22 *CMS Newsletter*, No. 327, May 1969.

23 *CMS Newsletter*, No. 327.

24 'The Ephesian Moment' in Andrew Walls, *The Cross-Cultural Process in Christian History* (Maryknoll, NY: Orbis, 2002), p. 78.

25 Walls, *The Cross-Cultural Process*, p. 79.

26 *CMS Newsletter*, No. 299, December 1966.

27 *CMS Newsletter*, No. 299.

28 *CMS Newsletter*, No. 357, February 1972.

29 *CMS Newsletter*, No. 329, July 1969.

30 *CMS Newsletter*, No. 329. Italics in original.

31 *CMS Newsletter*, No. 387, December 1974.

32 *CMS Newsletter*, No. 387.

33 *CMS Newsletter*, No. 387.

34 *CMS Newsletter*, No. 387.

35 *CMS Newsletter*, No. 279, February 1965.

36 Travel Diaries, Pakistan, Nepal, Afghanistan, Moscow, 1968, p. 107.

37 Travel Diaries, Pakistan, Nepal, Afghanistan, Moscow, 1968, p. 176.

38 Travel Diaries, USA 1970, p. 10.

39 Travel Diaries, USA 1970. Underlining in original.

40 *CMS Newsletter*, No. 346, February 1971.

41 *CMS Newsletter*, No. 346.

42 *CMS Newsletter*, No. 346.

43 *CMS Newsletter*, No. 320, October 1968.

44 J. Mbiti, quoted in Tite Tiénou, 'Christian Theology in an Era of World Christianity', in Craig Ott and Harold A. Netland (eds), *Globalizing Theology: Belief and practice in an era of world Christianity* (Ada, MI: Baker Academic, 2006), p. 45.

45 *CMS Newsletter*, No. 336, March 1970.

46 *CMS Newsletter*, No. 326, quotation by Brahmabandhab Upadhyaya.

47 *CMS Newsletter*, No. 326.

48 *CMS Newsletter*, No. 326.

49 *CMS Newsletter*, No. 297, October 1966.

50 *CMS Newsletter*, No. 326, April 1969.

51 *CMS Newsletter*, No. 326. Quoting from *The Expository Times*.

52 *CMS Newsletter*, No. 382, June 1974.

53 *CMS Newsletter*, No. 295, July 1966.

54 *CMS Newsletter*, No. 382, June 1974.

55 See for example Stephen Johnson, *Where Good Ideas Come From* (London: Allen Lane, 2010), p. 152.

56 Will Gompertz, *Think Like an Artist* (London: Penguin Random House, 2015), p. 96.

57 Roger Von Oech, *A Whack on the Side of the Head* (New York, NY: Warner Books, 1983), has 'that's not my area' as one of his mental blocks to creative thinking.

58 Robert Poynton, *Do Improvise* (London: The Do Book Company, 2013), p. 15.

4

Cherish the Weakness of Limited Means

The other side of the lake

Is there any need for mission organizations or communities in today's world, and if so, how are they best organized to be dynamic and responsive so that they remain movements rather than bogged down as institutions? Many of these organizations were set up to share Christ with those who did not know him in other cultures and countries. Now there are churches in many of those places. As we have already articulated, mission is best led by the locals. Local people are the natural leaders of mission into the future. This was always the vision of CMS from very early on. Henry Venn, General Secretary of CMS in the first half of the nineteenth century, sought to clarify the main goal of mission and the most effective means of achieving it. He mooted the idea of the indigenous church with the development of the three-self theory. A church was judged to be indigenous when it was self-propagating, self-financing, and self-governing. Here is how he puts it:

> The object of the Church Missionary Society's mission is the development of native churches with a view to their ultimate settlement upon a self-supporting, self-governing, and self-extending system. When this settlement has been effected the mission will have attained its euthanasia and all missionary agency transferred to the regions beyond.[1]

We endorse and support this approach to mission thinking and practice. We only wish it had been done more consistently!

This approach sharpens the focus for an organization like CMS. Its role is not to do everything but to be a community of people in mission who are always looking to the region beyond. One of the metaphors we use for this is 'the other side of the lake'. This draws on Jesus' mission in Mark 4.35—5.20. Here Jesus has been teaching a crowd in a highly successful ministry and then he says to the disciples, 'Let's go to the other side of the lake.' The other side of the lake is now Jordan and in Jesus' day would have been Syria. It's Gentile territory. It seems to be a crazy idea. Yet they go there and as is often the case with a journey to the new, they go through a storm on the way, which is perhaps also a sign of what is to come. On the other side is a graveyard with a demon-possessed man whom Jesus heals. However, Jesus emphatically does not allow him to come back with the disciples to join the Jewish culture and to be discipled. Instead this restored man remains in his own community and he becomes the natural leader to share the good news of what has happened to him with the others there. We like to think that this could be the founding of the Church in Syria through this 'fringe-dweller'.[2] Later, Jesus does return to this region where there is a huge hunger to hear what he has to say.

Is there always another side of the lake? If all of the lakes have been crossed then perhaps mission organizations are no longer needed. However, it is pretty clear that there are still many lakes to cross! In our training with pioneer students they are invariably seeing something that is beyond the edges of where the Church is – whether that be geographical or with particular groups and networks of people. We believe that there are still plenty of lakes to cross not only in our own context but also overseas, where there are great challenges and the need to cross borders and to be at the fringes. This is the focus of mission organizations. It is not to do the organizing and pastoral work – what some used to call diocesanization. That is important work but it is not the task of the mission organization.

However, this does also raise an interesting question – does every church need mission organizations or communities to call her across the lake? We believe that it is essential because eventually church structures nearly always focus inwards on themselves. When times are tough or there are financial difficulties, it is often mission that gets restructured or cut. Therefore mission organizations and communities have a prophetic role to continue to call the Church to mission beyond its own boundaries.

These mission communities can lead by practice. Our experience through the pioneer training at CMS has validated this. Many dioceses have a vision and strategy for mission but they often struggle to know how to resource it. They are not quite sure how it fits into their structures. It can go well but sadly we have many stories of pioneers struggling in these contexts. Many of our students have found it a relief and a release to belong to a community whose aim and calling is to go to the other side of the lake. They tell us that they have found a home at CMS because they have found a people and a context in which they can live out their calling.

In the landscape we are exploring in this book this is an essential part of the Church's forest or ecosystem. CMS has birthed both churches and mission movements in Africa and Asia. This means that there is the dual dynamic not only of essential church structures but also of the prophetic expressions that look, lead and call outwards. John Taylor has some great wisdom around how mission organizations can remain true to who they are and avoid getting bogged down as institutions. This is what we will explore in this chapter.

Secrets for mission movements

Institutions are important. It is easy to set up some sort of rhetoric that sounds as if they are bad and that we simply need free-flowing movements. We know that is unrealistic. However, it is worth reflecting on how institutions might retain a lightness of being. Why is it that institutions so often get stuck in bureaucracy and become bloated with hierarchy, regulations and self-importance? How do they remain light on their feet, able to reshape and reinvigorate themselves to remain viable and alive? Recently we have seen household names struggle to remain viable. Institutions and empires do not last for ever, so it is helpful to reflect on this.

John Taylor was keen to resist the settler impetus – the urge to settle down, to become so deeply established that lightness of touch and moving on become difficult, horizons become limited by too much stability, and attentiveness to the present, imagination and risk are sidelined. Shortly after becoming General Secretary, he reflected on the possibility for an organization such as CMS, which was once a movement, to recapture that vitality. He used organic and arboreal imagery to express this and wrote of the need to push out new shoots that will 'bud into fresh forms of experimentation and response'.[3] Likewise, his immediate predecessor, Max Warren, in his booklet *Iona and Rome* identified CMS with the wild spirit of Columba and Iona, suggesting that human nature prefers to be settled and organized by the church structures (Rome), rather than being disturbed by Iona.[4]

Taylor offers us five 'secrets of rejuvenation' that can help an organization to recover enough movement to stay alive. We believe that these 'secrets' are helpful for us today.[5]

His first secret relates to goals and purposes. Anyone who starts a movement has a clear and simple aim. However, as soon as a movement begins to be established and becomes more organized, inevitably a variety of aims and purposes will develop. Establishment and organization can lead to bureaucracy, compromise and an inherent conservatism. Taylor suggests that if we want to retain any hope of being and remaining a movement, we need to keep our aim limited and focused. According to Max Warren, the purpose of mission societies is evangelistic mission led largely by lay people who are a family and who are a 'fellowship of enthusiasts' ignited by a zeal from God.[6] We need to remain committed to our goal and purpose to avoid any unwieldy bureaucracy.

Taylor's second secret relates to leadership. He contends that for leadership to remain grassroots and creative it should be shared by as many people as possible. He is also keen on drawing in younger people and giving them responsibility. This is a plea that is heard in many boards around the UK but it seems difficult to put into practice! These days, we also need to increase our ethnic diversity on boards. A recent government-commissioned Report indicated that ethnic and cultural diversity is lagging behind some improvements in gender diversity on boards.[7]

Research indicates that a diversity of voices will lead to greater creativity. 'Diversity enhances creativity. It encourages the search for novel information and perspectives, leading to better decision making and problem solving ... Even simply being exposed to diversity can change the way you think.'[8]

As an organization grows and becomes more specialized it seems that leadership begins to be concentrated in fewer and fewer hands. Therefore, in order to keep a sense of common involvement, commitment and participation, Taylor urges trying to keep the organization small. This is counter-intuitive and a challenge, especially when church growth receives such an emphasis.

The third secret discusses power and resources. Of course, any organization needs both in order to function, but these can become temptations in themselves. Taylor's suggestion for avoiding this is to remain a movement, because a movement is always focused on achieving its aim, while an institution tends to accumulate power and capitalize it, which then leads to a burgeoning and potentially sluggish bureaucracy. In order to retain movement and initiative, he suggests that it is vital to 'cherish the weakness of limited means'.[9] Then the temptation to wield power and to collect capital is minimized. This is a challenge to the Church of England, in particular, which over the centuries has accumulated massive assets and property and developed a clericalized bureaucracy. Perhaps if the Church had been able to sit more lightly to both power and resources, we might look less like a multinational with assets, property portfolios and investment managers and more like a movement whose founder eschewed worldly power and resources. Limited means also has the beneficial side-effect that we have to trust and rely on God rather than our own resources. It forces us to be creative and innovative, imaginative and responsible as we work with 'the weakness of limited means' rather than limitless resources. It also puts us in line with most of the rest of the world, which is familiar with the reality of limited means.

Taylor's fourth secret relates to the distribution of functions. When a movement starts, the pioneer tends to do everything. However, as it grows it is important to share the vision, the tasks and the knowledge. Just as it is important to share the leadership widely, so it is helpful to distribute the functions widely and to break up any attempt at omnicompetence, power and control.

The fifth secret relates to overhauling the structures, and here Taylor unashamedly critiques the Church. He believes that our church structures and manner of organization actually hinder the Church from getting the Gospel out into the world, because church has become stuck – too parochial, inward-looking and clerical. He hates hearing clergy talk about 'my congregation' and believes this is quite wrong. He questions the parish structure and endorses 'little congregations' as new forms of missionary presence that have emerged in many places – among students, migrant workers and refugees, for example. Taylor believes that this kind of witness needs a team approach, so his fifth secret is to trust the team with full responsibility, initiative and vision.[10] We believe that this is precisely why mission organizations are needed.

These five secrets are Taylor's ideas on how to help an institution remain a movement. So often the weight of an institution seems to focus in on itself. It becomes drawn into its own affairs, focused on keeping itself going, keeping the show on the road; maintenance rather than movement, embracing the settler impulse.

A seminal article by missiologist Ralph Winter may be helpful here.[11] He writes about *modality* and *sodality*. Historically he likens modality to the diocese and sodality to the Roman Catholic orders such as the Benedictines and Franciscans. He believes that both modality and sodality are needed in the ecology or landscape of church. He gives the example of

Gregory the Great, head of a modality as bishop of the diocese of Rome, calling on Augustine to undertake his mission to England. Gregory called upon the sodality, which at this time was the Benedictine monastery, and asked Augustine and his members to undertake this dangerous journey and mission on his behalf. By the nineteenth century Winter cites the voluntary Protestant mission societies as examples of sodal movements. 'The vehicle that allowed the Protestant movement to become vital was the structural development of the sodality, which harvested the vital "voluntarism" latent in Protestantism, and surfaced in new mission agencies of all kinds, both at home and overseas.'[12] The modal tends to be more focused on the one place, on stability and rootedness, while the sodal has a more outward focus and an emphasis on exploration and pushing the boundaries. The energy of the Church in mission works best when it has both structures.

It is the sodal that prevents the modal from becoming too inward-looking and self-obsessed. CMS is an example of a sodal organization. Max Warren explains that CMS came into existence as a voluntary association 'to discharge a missionary obligation which the church as represented by its leaders did not even acknowledge'.[13] He goes on to outline some of the distinctive characteristics of CMS. It is voluntary in character, it is lay in character, it draws on wells of spirituality from revival traditions, there is a deep corporate sense of commitment and devotion to a common task, and the primary responsibility of a mission agency is evangelism.[14] This recalls some of Taylor's secrets around maintaining a focused aim, and volunteers providing and sharing in the power, resources and functions.

Warren freely acknowledges the problem of 'church maintenance' both at home and overseas, and insists on the necessity for a 'forward evangelistic movement rather than emphasis on consolidation'.[15] This is where the sodal can help us by maintaining this focus on movement, on pushing out to the edges, by being involved in a wider world, and by going to the other side of the lake. The sodal knows that our faith is a boundary-crossing faith and that is when it is most alive. If we remain only in Christian environments or institutions, our faith wanes and becomes static. It is most enlivened, challenged and renewed in the border-crossing encounters.

Taylor's challenge is how to keep on moving, crossing borders, moving to the edges. We have found that it is at the edges that creativity can thrive and new ideas be brought to birth. Taylor's arboreal imagery explores this and picks up the idea of pushing to the edge:

> The fresh nursery plantling grows into a tree. Must it then deplore the hardness of its bark, the fixity of its roots, the intricacy of its branches? Is new life to be found only in the seedlings it scatters on the surrounding soil? As long as the tree lasts, its real growth is to be found in the fresh buds which season after season push out from the tough timber. If you are concerned with movement and growth in a church or in a society, look to the fringes. Watch the things that are pushing out on the edge.[16]

Institutional power as humility

It is important to acknowledge that a mission organization such as CMS has and leverages power. Although CMS positions itself on the edge of the Church of England and is a Voluntary Association, it is also an Acknowledged Community of the Church of England. This gives it a certain amount of power, privilege and status. Of course, these are realities and it is not easy or perhaps even possible to deny them or give them up, but it is possible to acknowledge them and to be aware of how these realities colour our view of the world and our mission engagement. For example, gender, ethnicity and diversity audits have made us aware of how these imbalances in an organization can skew policies and appointments, and how white, male privilege has, for so long, been the norm.[17] Taylor is realistic enough to know that an organization such as CMS, founded in 1799, has indeed become an institution, with all the accretions and complexities that this implies.

In order to try to counter this and to maintain the impetus

towards the margins, Taylor reveals a sixth 'secret', which is *'humility and poverty of spirit'*.[18] Humility and poverty of spirit will ensure that an institution does not take itself too seriously and will be aware of its own needs and failings. It will know that humility, hiddenness and poverty are profoundly Christian values because this is what Jesus modelled in the incarnation – *kenosis* or emptying himself to live among us.

By contrast, so much of our current institutional thinking is focused on the drive for growth, expansion, projects, strategies and numbers. We have targets to meet, business plans to write, strategies to elaborate, conversions to count, projects to develop. Much of this language and worldview comes from the worlds of the military and management – worlds of war and success. In fact there is even a term, 'managerial missiology' – a cold, reductionist term turning Christian mission into a manageable enterprise using information technology and marketing techniques. Concepts and programmes such as the '10–40' and the '4–14' window, 'Adopt-a-People', 'homogeneous units' come from this approach. Peruvian missiologist Samuel Escobar offers the following critique, 'What I am seeing in the application of these concepts in the mission field is that missionaries "depersonalize" people into "unreached targets", making them objects of hit-and-run efforts to get decisions that may be reported.'[19] Where is the language that expresses our mission engagement in terms of weakness, vulnerability, relationships, service, compassion, meekness? Where is the language and where are the practices that express our institutional thinking in terms of 'humility and poverty of spirit'?

We resonate with the three qualities of mind that Taylor suggests are needed to maintain humility and retain movement.[20]

1 First, 'mobility, the spirit which welcomes change as the breath of life, which allows the situation to dictate the terms, and knows that the present matters more than the past'. This quality is desperately needed today when so many of our churches seem stuck in the past – both in their architecture and in their ways of relating to society. Think of the many Anglican churches one enters, only to be assaulted

by damp and mildew, dusty hymn books, rolls of old flip charts stacked in the corner, and a general air of something tired, dated and not much loved. Where is the humility and courage to listen to the present, to see this through fresh eyes, and to discern the issues that people care about?

2 The second quality is one Taylor describes with a newly minted word, 'picnicity – a preference for travelling light as if on a permanent picnic, knowing that what matters is the person, not the possessions; conviction, not convention'. The ability to travel light, not to be cluttered by possessions both personal and bureaucratic, is clearly linked to material poverty, as well as to a poverty of spirit.

3 The third one is 'particularity. This means a particular group or association striving to be all that it is meant to be, and to do only what it is meant to do.' Again we like this emphasis on keeping the focus as an absolute priority.

These three ideas of mobility, picnicity and particularity can help an institution act in humility as it travels lightly, knows and remains focused on its particular calling, and has the courage to live that out. These are also qualities that exercise appeal today when so many people are striving to live a life that honours the present and to live in the local, to minimize their carbon footprint, to cherish the earth and strangers, and to live a life that is lighter and freer of possessions and encumbrances.

Change, dissent and refounding

How does newness come when institutions get stuck? There is considerable writing on organizations and change management, and also on how organizations can create healthy environments for innovation. One writer we have found really helpful in our own thinking about this is anthropologist Gerald Arbuckle. He writes about change as dissent:

> There can be no constructive change at all, even in church, unless there is some form of dissent. By dissent I mean

simply the proposing of alternatives, and a system that is not continuously examining alternatives is not likely to evolve creatively.[21]

Arbuckle is a member of a spread-out religious community in the Roman Catholic Church and he believes that religious communities are the sodal structures or prophetic communities in the Church able to see and propose alternatives to the status quo. It is worth noting that these communities are themselves part of the Church.

Taylor was aware of this and did not want CMS to lose its missionary purpose. 'The one who is engaged in church-work or in a church institution is tempted to grow too churchly; wholly concerned with making church members more holy or efficient.'[22] He suggested the founding of 'A Brotherhood of Commitment', whose purpose would be to encourage a more sustained commitment to missionary obedience together than can be sustained as individuals. He was aware that this would be a new thing, potentially a radical approach, and that it would need careful developing,

> We shall be pioneering a pattern which must apply to married as well to single, without any hint of a double standard. We must look for a form of devotional life which will make those who follow it more, and not less, secular, for we must be true to our calling as a lay movement.[23]

This 'Brotherhood of Commitment' appears to be the fore-runner to CMS becoming an Acknowledged Community of the Church of England in 2008.

Wise leaders, whether of businesses, churches or communities, know that as well as good faithful leaders of the core business they need to create spaces for dissent and innovation and to encourage those who carry this gift. This can go well if dissenters are able to be networked or be in groups together. Institutions that are able to encourage dissent remain healthy, dynamic and alive. They can resist conformity and embrace change of direction where necessary.

We need a kind of missiology of resistance and prophetic

dissent that will undermine power, resist domination and encourage a healthy dissent. To engage in a missiology of resistance we need support: we need a community around us who will support, encourage, pray and stand alongside us. Again, that is why mission structures are so helpful when they work well. Over the centuries, CMS has attempted to engage in prophetic dissent, from its early involvement in the abolition of the slave trade, its resistance to cruel sports such as bear baiting, up to the present day, with mission partners campaigning against female genital mutilation, or for a living wage for cleaners in London. We also find that the pioneer students identify very much with the notion of prophetic dissent as articulated in this way. Resistance and dissent enable a kind of prophetic imagination and posture that can highlight issues of injustice, encourage analysis and evaluation and provoke change. Along with change comes hope – that it does not always have to be like this; that a new world is possible.

Related to the notion of dissent is the idea of refounding. Refounding, a term used by Arbuckle, is a return to the founding story or experience of a community or organization such as the Church, the NHS, or CMS, connecting with the energy of it back in its day, re-owning it and then creatively applying that to today's most urgent needs. It is a drive to the heart or roots of a tradition, sometimes reclaiming it over and against itself in order to break open newness in the present.

Arbuckle explains that a church must always be in reformation because it will be confronting different situations and contexts from those for which it was founded. This resonates with Taylor's idea of mobility and 'the spirit which welcomes change as the breath of life', and paying attention to the present. This may mean having the courage to tear down old structures and cultural habits when they are no longer appropriate for the current context. This may be a painful process, a chaotic process. Passing through chaos may mean suffering. But it is a necessary process if we are to rediscover our aim and purpose, our focus, our original story and relive it in the present. It may be like passing through the storm and going to the other side of the lake.

Moreover, Arbuckle insists that it is not councils or committees that help to refound but rather a prophetic person, a dissenter. He gives some of the Old Testament prophets as examples; they simultaneously criticized the people for the gap between the vision of who they were and the reality of who they had become, but also energized the people to bridge that gap through faith by giving them hope. They exercised creative imagination. He writes that 'dissenters reframe things we take for granted by offering new ways of viewing issues or by putting them into contexts that we did not previously think possible. Dissenters expand our imaginations.'[24]

Dissenters are committed to hard work. They are committed to small beginnings. They tolerate failure. And they are community-oriented; like the prophets before them. They engage in what we might call faithful improvisation. The challenge for the institution is to give permission for this, not to quench the refounding impulse and creative imagination of the refounder but to allow this creative urge to flourish. This can be a challenge for institutions that fear change and innovation because it is pushing the boundaries into newness and the unknown. Arbuckle reminds us that 'cultures have an inbuilt resistance to change and will normally do everything possible to obstruct the fear-creating alternatives of dissenters. The Church, like any organization or culture, cannot escape this dilemma.'[25] For an institution to thrive, we believe that it must continually be refounding itself in order to remain true to its aim and purpose, or it will die or become seriously unfaithful to its calling. This is a challenging reminder not only for mission organizations that need to refound but also for church denominations and dioceses.

Taylor engages in questions of refounding in several newsletters. He is constantly asking what is the role of a mission society in this era. He is certain that the role of the mission society 'is no longer what it used to be, not what we thought it was. Yet we continue to talk and write about it in terms that are no longer valid.'[26] He gives a powerful example of this by providing a fascinating analysis of the kind of missionaries that CMS has sent overseas during the last 200 years. The initial missionaries were practical men (and, at first, they were indeed all men) – carpenters, weavers, builders, 'who never eclipsed but rather encouraged the incipient leadership of their converts. So by the middle of the nineteenth century, the churches which they had built in Africa and Asia were already beginning to look truly indigenous.'[27] However, at the same time CMS was beginning to receive applications from men with university degrees, graduates and highly-trained professionals, which may have enriched the forms of service offered but had unfortunate, and possibly unforeseen, consequences. These men slowed down the development of a truly indigenous church, 'by setting more finicky and formal criteria for judging the "readiness" of a Church to manage its own affairs'.[28] The impulse to impose Western standards and Western ways of doing things was too strong. Missionaries were, wittingly or unwittingly, bearers of British influence. The missionary also meant money. Even where the missionary had made considerable sacrifices, they were still rich in the eyes of their African and Asian neighbours at that time. And even if they were not, they were still representatives of an external source of funds and power. Taylor readily acknowledged that some of this is stereotype and generalization and that when Africans and Asians speak of individual missionaries they speak fondly of friends whom they have loved. However, 'when it is the *genus* missionary that is under discussion an image of foreignness and domination reasserts itself. It is something we have to live with, and by the grace of God, to live down.'[29]

Taylor's ideas offer us an excellent example of the urgent need for CMS to refound, to remember its founding story but to reimagine and improvise what that means and looks like in a new era. If institutions are unable to practise refounding, then they become stuck and unable to reinvent themselves in order to remain faithful to their original purpose in a new context and era.

Asking radical questions and taking risks

The ability to ask radical questions means that an institution will continually have to reimagine its role and purpose in the world. The last 50 years have been challenging for the Church in the West, with stories of decline and pressure as she tries to adapt to a fast-changing world. There have been examples of dissent and experimentation through the asking of difficult questions and the taking of risks. In the UK this has been exemplified by Fresh Expressions of Church. This book could be seen as part of that ongoing conversation. The reason for riffing on John Taylor is that there is so much wisdom to draw on. As General Secretary in a postcolonial world, Taylor began to see the winds of change and could detect that Western power and influence were on the wane. He asserted that CMS must be ready to face some radical and tough questions.

He narrated a powerful parable to illustrate neo-colonial approaches to mission:

> A couple with twelve children lived wretchedly in two rooms for which they paid an exorbitant rent. One of the landlord's daughters, who had never been encouraged to know about her father's business affairs, had taken a kindly interest in two of the poor children, bringing them toys and reading them Bible stories when they were little, giving them holidays in the country and later, paying their fees at a private boarding school. But one day the poor parents were bold enough to speak their mind. 'Lady', they said, 'instead of alienating two of our children, treat us as a family and, if you really want to help, get your own father to give us a fair deal. Otherwise, keep out!'[30]

He used this parable to describe the importance of seeing ourselves as others see us and for CMS to reflect on its role and approach to mission. Taylor did not duck the hard issues of power, colonialism, vested interests, poverty and wealth, patronage and patriarchy – all of which are found in this parable. His analysis of the structures of domination implicit in neocolonialism is what it means to engage in resistance and dissent and to ask radical questions about CMS's mission involvement and how to reassess it.

He was one of the first missiologists and mission leaders to understand that mission is from everywhere to everywhere and not just from the West to the rest. 'We are at last coming to understand that the frontiers and the problems and the methods of mission are the same the world over.'[31] That approach to mission would have far-reaching implications for the self-understanding of CMS and its members. He was acknowledging that mission was also needed at home – a radical concept in the 1960s! He repeatedly emphasized that Britain is a 'field for mission as needy as Asia or Africa' and so he implored CMS to offer 'a fresh and humbler image of its mission to stir the imagination and enlist the service of a new generation'.[32]

Moreover Taylor believed that all CMS members are engaged in the same mission, whether they are working overseas as designated missionaries or remaining at home as Christians committed to the same missionary enterprise. This removed the mystique from the concepts associated with the word 'missionary' and made every Christian disciple responsible for mission. This meant a real commitment to discipleship and a questioning of previous convictions and ways of doing things.

This understanding of mission helped to fuel *Mission-Shaped Church*, Fresh Expressions of Church and pioneering, as we understand that mission is everyone's responsibility.

These examples demonstrate that asking radical questions is a gift for an institution or an organization because it can breathe fresh life and new ideas into ageing structures. That is why we are asking questions in this book that may seem shocking, such as whether church is something that we leave or that is imagined very differently.

Risk-taking is very much linked to asking radical questions. The Church can sometimes seem to promote quite a risk-averse culture. How do we become more daring and open to risk and experimentation? CMS, from its very founding, had to take risks. One of CMS's founding principles in 1799 was what was known as the Church principle and not the High Church principle. This meant that it was to be loyal to the Church of England but also voluntary by its association and not dominated by the clergy – it encouraged the participation of lay people. Another early challenge was that no English men offered to go as the first missionaries, so CMS had to risk sending foreigners and lay people! By 1813 twelve Germans had been sent to West Africa and the first three English laymen were on their way to New Zealand. Yet another risk was gaining acceptance from the institutional church. It took 18 months to get some sort of acceptance from the Archbishop of Canterbury, but it was not until 1815 that official Church of England approval was given by a bishop. The very founding of CMS as a mission society was a risky, fragile venture and undertaking.

It is important for an institution to keep on taking risks, otherwise it will become domesticated and ultimately die. We believe that we need to take more risks, to experiment and to see what might be possible. Ultimately God calls us to take risks just as God took the ultimate risk in the incarnation.

Letting go and living with ambiguity

For institutions and structures to stay engaged and relevant, they have to practise letting go and learning to live with ambiguity. While they have to know their 'particularity' or focus, they also have to know what to let go in order to continue to function and be faithful to their calling in their current context. For example, Taylor was aware that the days of long-term mission service overseas might no longer be appropriate for CMS. This is because the task of mission is the primary responsibility of local Christians, 'Christians on the spot'.[33] It might be time for the Western mission agency to let go and let them get on with it. He lamented in strong terms that:

> For half a century we have been treating our fellow Christians in Asia and Africa as young colonies of the Home Church rather than as partners in the world mission. We have allowed overseas dioceses to feel we were there because *they*

needed *us* rather than because mankind [sic] needed Christ. No wonder they long to do without us![34]

Although this was written in 1963, we wonder what churches overseas would say to this today. Might they still resonate with this?

Taylor insisted that our missionary volunteering should not undermine, but rather must encourage, a volunteering and innovative spirit in the local churches. It is too easy for the missionary to take over and lead, thereby squashing any local initiative and ideas and more appropriately contextual ways of doing things. He also insisted that we must follow the way of the incarnated Christ by being among the poor. Imagine if the Church were able to let go of old ways of doing things and become a Church that 'cherishes the value of limited means'.[35] Imagine if we were able to trust the local because mission is the responsibility of Christians on the spot. He asserted:

We should be concerned with the making of plans, not so much *for* as *with* the poor, and that involves living with them. This may suggest a different sort of milieu for some of our missionaries in order that, as a Society, we may more naturally understand poverty and powerlessness.[36]

Taylor was always aware of issues of power and he advocated withdrawing from any ministry that 'seems inescapably to collude in maintaining the privileged position of the elite', citing 'snob' congregations or exclusive schools as examples.[37] He understood the power dynamics inherent in the work of mission agencies and he exhorted them 'to examine much more critically their own (probably unconscious) involvement in the power structures of the wealthy nations and to re-order their relationships with the Churches of the Third World more radically and more quickly than they have so far done'.[38]

This is a hard call because it means letting go – letting go of our power and privilege, letting go of our entitlements (and our titles!), our place in the world, letting go of our resources and our lifestyle, letting go of our sense of superiority. We need to practise more listening, more solidarity with and being alongside. These attitudes and postures would be signs of an institution that is able to practise letting go.

The current climate in the charity sector and indeed the wider church is concerned with sharpness of focus, purpose, vision and impact. There is nothing wrong with those things in and of themselves, but we observe what appears to be an obsession with counting and measurement to prove success. A sort of skewing can arise from that, because it is much harder to prove and measure success on the other side of the lake. This can then lead to finding easier and more measurable outcomes. By way of a counterbalance we think it is important for institutions to learn to live with ambiguity. It can imply uncertainty but it can also imply that something works on many levels – is multivalent or multi-layered. Jesus exhibited this in his teaching, and especially in his parables, which were often ambiguous. They work on various levels and there are many ways of reading them and locating oneself in them. Ambiguity can intrigue and allow for spaces to open up. Ambiguity encourages us not to ring fence or to create boundaries but rather to be open to what might emerge if we are willing to sit with the ambiguous. Mission in the contexts of different faiths is a very good example of this, as explored in Chapter 6.

Fringe-dwellers

Taylor is a fan of looking to the fringes, crossing boundaries, watching what is pushing out at the edges. This is where new ideas can emerge and can infiltrate organizations to revive and renew them. We think that crossing over to the other side of the lake and pioneering are good metaphors for this approach – always looking beyond, yearning to listen and learn from the edges, experimenting with the new while respecting the old. We want to resist the settler impulse and not become too established. We want to maintain our focus, our mobility, our 'picnicity'. We want to cherish the value of limited means. We endeavour to practise humility and poverty of spirit. We value dissent and welcome the asking of questions and the taking of risks. We want to keep moving, being renewed by encounter and challenge. We want to be able to let go, to live with ambiguity and to continue to be disturbed by the wild Spirit of God. We hope that this impetus will keep pushing us to the other side of the lake.

Exercising Creativity

Dreaming space

The best and certainly the most fun book on creativity in relation to institutional life must surely be *Orbiting the Giant Hairball*.[39] Gordon MacKenzie worked as a creative at Hallmark Cards for 30 years. He uses the metaphor of an institution's processes and bureaucracy being like a giant hairball that is easy to get stuck in. Institutions are a gift and we need them but he says that for the creative, the key is resisting the pull of Corporate Gravity and finding a way to orbit where the air is clear round the edges, beyond the hairball of the corporate mindset, with responsible creativity that is still connected to the spirit of the corporate mission. He says, 'During those 30 years there was not a day when I was not subject to the inexorable pull of Corporate Gravity tug, tug, tugging me toward (and during one unhappy year right into) the tangle of the Hairball where the ghosts of past successes outvote original thinking.'[40] This tension exists in every organization and is what Taylor is getting at when he yearns for structures that enable operating as a movement rather than giving in to the settler impulse. In the pioneer training we experience this challenge as we seek to orbit two giant hairballs of a university and a denomination (three if you include CMS)! So how do you find the thin air that MacKenzie is talking about?

'Imagination is the most precious thing you have got as

a creative', according to Jane Rapley.[41] She uses the metaphor of a bank and says that there is a problem if we keep spending without putting money in. You go into overdraft or the money stops. So you have to keep feeding it.

As discussed earlier, the kind of team atmosphere that is created is critical. Does it celebrate imagination and creativity? Then there are practices that can help. One we have found really good is to have dreaming spaces two or three times a year. For these we book somewhere away from the office, usually for 24 hours with an overnight stay. We pick a focus for the dreaming – for example, pioneering mission and business. And we simply explore this focus in playful fashion with lots of good food and conversation and scribbling of pictures and ideas. While it is relevant to our work, we try and keep it not too agenda-driven. Invariably we find that ideas and actions emerge that end up shaping future direction. Usually we have a mix of team and students. Retreat, rest, good holidays, days out of the office, visits to other spaces and cultures, networking, extended study leave are other practices that lend themselves to breathing thin air.

One of the puzzles of creativity is where ideas come from. Edward de Bono suggests that not enough attention is paid to that because of what he terms 'logic in hindsight'.[42] In other words, once someone has come up with an idea, when you look back it seems obvious so we assume it was logical beforehand, which is very rarely the case. He says, 'An idea may be logical in hindsight but invisible in foresight.'[43] One thing is for sure – if you sit down to focus on coming up with an idea you probably won't! In a survey in the Stress Report the two highest scoring activities for where people come up with ideas are exercise and the shower.[44] Walking or staring out of the window, rest even, are so helpful for clearing the mind and daydreaming. Switching off headphones, TV and social media will help as they easily rob us of that sort of space.[45] It is also helpful to play, whatever your kind of play is. We find visiting exhibitions and gigs, engaging with poets, writers and artists a sort of play that invariably sparks our own ideas. In our efficiency-driven and measurement-obsessed organizations playing or finding headspace doesn't score too highly, so it requires a determination to create space for those practices and value them.

Creativity is catching, so it's good practice to hang around people who love ideas and imagination. Curiosity and getting outside your areas, as discussed previously, are also key so that you can borrow or steal other ideas.[46] Steve Johnson researched where good ideas come from and two findings of his that we particularly like are the slow hunch and the adjacent possible.[47] He says that lots of people assume that an idea is a eureka moment, a flash in the pan. But often people have an idea that percolates as a hunch for a long time before it comes into being. That is the slow hunch. Then he also suggests that when a discovery is made through an exploration it is like going into a room in which there are several new doors that are now possible to go through – the adjacent possible. So, for example, the idea that we might conceive of mission in the UK as cross-cultural, drawing on insights from cross-cultural mission overseas, has led into a room that has exploded all sorts of adjacent possibilities. This is why resisting the settler impulse, as Taylor puts it, is so important.

Paradoxically, creativity can be helped by limits. The show *Whose Line Is It Anyway* is a good example of this, where the actors are given constraints to improvise with and within. How many incredible songs have been written with 'three chords and the truth'? Ideas are free, so for mission organizations being encouraged to 'cherish the weakness of limited means' should be a catalyst for imagination rather than a source of concern.

Exercises

1   Organize a 24-hour dreaming space with a small group or your team. Pick a theme related to your mission but not something too front and centre in the corporate strategy. Then dream together. Make sure you have someone who will record the flow of the conversation through note taking or photographing things created. Circulate the notes to all participants after the dreaming space.

2   Who do you know in your organization that you think of as creative? Who do you think of in your organization as having the gift of dissent? Find a way to collaborate on a project with them. Hang around them. Enjoy their imagination. Notice how it makes you feel. Be curious and find out what makes them tick.

3   Write in your diary a time in work when you will do something that is thin air or headspace for you. Go for a long walk. Book a retreat. Work at home but don't fill it with doing emails or spreadsheets or reports. Note down in a journal afterwards any thoughts or ideas or connections that you had or made.

4   What are the limited means in your mission organization, church, or area of work in your team? How can you cherish them? Imagine you are on a programme of *Whose Line Is It Anyway* and are given those resources with which to improvise in line with your organization's mission. What could you come up with?

Notes

1 Quoted in Eugene Stock, *History of the Church Missionary Society, Vol II* (London: 1899), p. 83.

2 *CMS Newsletter*, No. 353, October 1971.

3 *CMS Newsletter*, No. 285, September 1965.

4 Max Warren, 'Iona and Rome, Being some Reflections on the Missionary Work of the Church of England prompted by a study of Canon Campbell McLeod's book entitled *Christian History in the Making*', *The Record*, 12, 19 and 26 July 1946.

5 Two of these secrets resonate with some of CMS's founding principles, two of which are: start small and put money in second place. See www.ampltd.co.uk/digital_guides/church_missionary_society_archive_general/editorial%20introduction%20by%20rosemary%20keen.aspx (accessed 7.8.2019).

6 Max Warren, 'Iona and Rome'.

7 The Parker Review, www.ey.com/uk/en/newsroom/news-releases/17-10-12-final-recommendations-of-the-parker-review-published (accessed 7.8.2019).

8 Katherine Phillips, 'How Diversity Makes Us Smarter', *Scientific American*, 1 October 2014, www.scientificamerican.com/article/how-diversity-makes-us-smarter/ (accessed 7.8.2019).

9 *CMS Newsletter*, No. 285, September 1965.

10 Two of these secrets resonate with some of CMS's founding principles, two of which are: start small, and put money in second place. See www.ampltd.co.uk/digital_guides/church_missionary_society_archive_general/editorial%20introduction%20by%20rosemary%20keen.aspx (accessed 7.8.2019).

11 Ralph Winter, 'The Two Structures of God's Redemptive Mission', *Missiology*, Vol. l2, Issue no. 1, 1974, pp. 121–39.

12 Winter, 'The Two Structures', p. 227.

13 Warren, 'Iona and Rome'.

14 Warren, 'Iona and Rome', pp. 11–14.

15 Warren, 'Iona and Roma', p. 19.

16 *CMS Newsletter*, No. 285, September 1965.

17 See Grayson Perry, *The Descent of Man* (London: Penguin, 2017).

18 *CMS Newsletter*, No. 285, September 1965. Italics in original.

19 S. Escobar, *The New Global Mission, The Gospel from Everywhere to Everywhere* (Downers Grove: InterVarsity Press, 2003), p. 167.

20 *CMS Newsletter*, No. 344, December 1970.

21 Gerald Arbuckle, *Refounding the Church: Dissent for Leadership* (London: Geoffrey Chapman, 1993), p. 1.

22 *CMS Newsletter*, No. 290, February 1966.

23 *CMS Newsletter*, No. 290.

24 Gerald Arbuckle, *Refounding*, p. 113.

25 Arbuckle, *Refounding*, p. 111.

26 *CMS Newsletter*, No. 302, March 1967.

27 *CMS Newsletter*, No. 302.

28 *CMS Newsletter*, No. 302.

29 *CMS Newsletter*, No. 302.

30 *CMS Newsletter*, No. 339, June 1970.

31 *CMS Newsletter*, No. 290, February 1966.

32 *CMS Newsletter*, No. 297, October 1966.

33 *CMS Newsletter*, No. 318, July 1968.

34 *CMS Newsletter*, No. 264, October 1963. Italics in original.

35 *CMS Newsletter*, No. 285, September 1965.

36 *CMS Newsletter*, No. 298, November 1966. Italics in original.

37 *CMS Newsletter*, No. 298.

38 *CMS Newsletter*, No. 370, April 1973.

39 Gordon Mackenzie, *Orbiting the Giant Hairball* (New York: Viking Penguin, 1998).

40 Mackenzie, *Orbiting*, p. 32.

41 Janet Rapley, in Bob and Roberta Smith, Edmund de Waal et al, *The Creative Stance* (London: Common Editions, 2016), p. 80.

42 Edward de Bono, *Teach Your Child to Think* (London: Penguin Books, 1993), p. 16.

43 de Bono, *Teach Your Child to Think*, p. 17.

44 David Hieatt, *The Stress Report* (London: The Do Lectures, 2016), p. 7.

45 See John Hegarty, *Hegarty on Creativity: There are No Rules* (London: Thames & Hudson, 2014), p. 58; Hieatt, *Stress Report*, pp. 103–4.

46 Austin Kleon, *Steal Like an Artist* (New York: Workman Publishing, 2012), pp. 2–23.

47 Stephen Johnson, *Where Good Ideas Come From* (London: Allen Lane, 2010), p. 21, p. 67.

PART THREE

Society

5

Enough is Enough!

Salvation is a story of the world

Mission is concerned with the world and its redemption and healing. God so loved this world that he gave his only Son. The 'world' means the cosmos, the incredible, beautiful, rainbow-rich creation that God has made. The earth, our home, one tiny planet spinning in space in the vastness of the universe, is extraordinary with its wonderful creatures, plants, landscapes and habitats. To gaze at the ocean's horizon, to walk in a forest and listen to birdsong, to climb a mountain, to sleep under a starry sky, to hold a newborn baby's tiny fingers in a hand, to enjoy a freshly cooked meal with friends, all evoke wonder and thankfulness. What a gift life is, what a gift it is to be alive! The Christian story is fundamentally a story about the world, the heavens and the earth that have been made good and entrusted to us as gift to look after with love, tenderness and care. That world is packed with potential to be developed, unfolded creatively with imagination in loving friendship with God the Creator whose very breath and Spirit sustain the universe. It's an amazing playground in which to develop ideas, to trade, to share in music, art, community, travel, architecture, farming, inventions, science, learning, to the glory of God. The first mission mandate is a cultural mandate to open up, to steward and take care of God's world.[1] John Taylor's way of putting it is simply to say that we are responsible for this planet before God.[2] That world can be opened up in ways that lead to life and blessing, or it can be opened up in ways that shut life down and lead to death or curses. Attentiveness to God's Spirit of wisdom and the wisdom of God's word will help us walk in the former ways.

And yet everything is broken. The world is fallen. There is a mystery to this captured in the story of Adam and Eve's disobedience, but we experience it in our very selves as well as in all areas of life. Opening up life is a struggle. That brokenness runs in and through all things. Whether we are raising children, running a business or farming, we experience both the goodness of life and the struggle. We long for healing, for redemption. The whole world is crying out for liberation from this bondage to decay.[3] The Christian story of redemption begins with God calling out a people to live in obedience to God's wisdom and ways, with a mix of chapters and episodes as they alternate between faithfulness and turning away to follow other gods. Following other gods seems attractive and they seem to promise much, but invariably following them leads to one disaster or another – famine, disease, slavery, war or exile. That in turn leads God's people to return and seek God afresh, to live in ways that lead to life. During this cycle there is a longing articulated by the prophets for a different order of redemption, for the one who will come finally to crush the evil in the world and who will somehow take on the brokenness of the world so that we might be healed through his woundedness. Jesus Christ is the Saviour of the world who fulfils that in his life, death and resurrection. Through him all things in heaven and on earth are reconciled to God. The scope of redemption is as wide as creation itself. When Christ returns there will be a renewed heavens and earth finally set free from brokenness so that there will be no more tears, no more sorrow, no more pain. This is a story of the world, of God's world.

When I was at university a friend who had recently become a Christian came to see me in tears. She was upset because while she loved Jesus she could not bear the idea of heaven. She had somehow picked up the idea that the Christian story was not about the world's healing and redemption but about its destruction and escaping from it. She pictured a future of wearing white sitting on a cloud and singing worship songs for ever. While being with God sounded wonderful, she loved the creation and it made no sense that it would be destroyed. She couldn't believe it when I said that the story she had been told was not the story of the Bible and that the future was a bodily earthly existence where presumably all the good things God has made would be enjoyed but without the struggle. I suggested that she should begin to imagine salvation as a story of the world and not one of escape from it. Christ's resurrection from the dead and the gift of the Holy Spirit are our hope and guarantee for that future (re)new(ed) heavens and earth. Hans Küng described the kingdom of God as creation healed.[4] That is as good a two-word summary of God's mission as any we have come across. To participate in mission therefore is to join in with that healing of all things with the gifts we have been given. We are to be lovers of God and lovers of God's good earth who are praying, living and working for its renewal and for God's kingdom to come on earth as it is in heaven.

Reducing the scope of salvation to something private, a restored personal relationship with God, or to a story of escape from this world as we receive a ticket to heaven, with this world being destroyed, has been a powerful myth that still circulates in sermons, hymns and popular theologies.[5] That dualism has led the Church in the West to prioritize issues of evangelism, church and private morality. While not universally true, its ripples have been huge. It has meant that the Church has been too slow to engage in public life and with 'worldly' concerns like money and greed, and with the environmental crisis of the planet itself. It is to these two deeply connected issues in society that we turn in this chapter – because they may just be the two most pressing mission concerns, and indeed society concerns, that we have right now.

Looking for alternative imagination

The intertwined crises of economics and the environment are rooted in greed and threaten the wellbeing and survival of humanity, living creatures and planet earth, our home.[6] Any serious look at the data shows that the issues are very real indeed. Data on wealth inequality and on the environment are equally shocking.

Scientists generally are somewhat cautious about sticking their necks out. So when 21,000 scientists from 184 countries co-signed an article in 2017 entitled 'World Scientists' Warning To Humanity: A Second Notice', making it the most supported journal article ever, you know they are concerned.[7] William Ripple, one of the authors, says that the job of scientists is to tell the truth and even though they are frustrated and in despair at inaction, they will continue to speak out on what needs to be done to protect life on planet earth.[8] This includes reducing population growth, consuming fewer fossil fuels, meat and other resources. Reports raising concern about the environment can be traced back to Rachel Carson's 1962 book, *Silent Spring*.[9] So it is certainly not news any more, which in some ways makes it all the more shocking how little has been done. The United Nations set up an Intergovernmental Panel on Climate Change (IPCC) which publishes research and reports on a regular basis and is seen to be the gold standard assessment of the state of the planet.[10] The big issue is global temperature rising due to carbon emissions. The last IPCC report suggested that there are 12 years left in which to change and limit warming to 1.5 degrees, which, as we are experiencing, is already having dramatic impact. David Wallace Wells' remarkable book, *The Uninhabitable Earth*, has over six pages of footnotes citing the evidence to back up his writing, in which he outlines the cascades taking place that will only accelerate as we reach that temperature and beyond. He opens the book with the ominous words, 'It is worse, much worse, than you think.'[11] Heat, rising oceans and flooding, large areas becoming uninhabitable, associated migrations, disease, so-called natural disasters, wildfires, economic collapse and conflict are some of the 12 mutually related threats that he explores in brutal fashion. He says that each of these on its own

> contains enough horror to induce a panic attack in the most optimistic of those considering it. But you are not merely

considering it, you are about to embark on living it. In many cases, in many places we already are.[12]

When it comes to wealth, 1 per cent of the world's population owns 50 per cent of the world's wealth. There are very powerful elites with vested interests who are unlikely to change business as usual. In spite of what we now know about global warming, the UK subsidises fossil fuel to the tune of 10.5 billion pounds a year, which is extraordinary.

It is amazing that John Taylor was reflecting on these two themes as long ago as 1972. He published a double-length newsletter entitled *Enough is Enough*[13] and went on to develop the ideas further in a book of the same name.[14] He gets straight to the heart of the matter when he says:

> Our Western way of life is marked by excess whichever aspect of our situation one looks at – our consumption of food and our accumulation of goods, our wage claims and price rises, our waste and pollution, the concentration and congestion of our cities, our destruction of living creatures and our plunder of fuels and minerals, our expenditure on armaments and the wanton disproportion of the way we use them – excess is the word that comes continually to mind. Ruthless, unbridled, unthinking excess.[15]

He gives four examples of our irresponsible excess, each of which is prescient and eerily current in our twenty-first century.

- His first example is our use of the private car. He sharply criticizes the indiscriminate use of the car and its use as a commuter vehicle that encourages the creation of distant dormitory suburbs and excessive air pollution.
- His second example concerns animal and marine life, with fishing, especially whales, as his particular focus. He attacks the unthinking callousness of the whale hunters and exclaims, 'To hunt any species to the point of extinction shows a kind of madness, for not only does that particular industry kill itself but a part of the richness of creation has been irreparably destroyed. And for what?'[16] He explains

that our unrestrained pillage of the seas threatens the extinction of many species.

- His third example is the casual toleration of industrial pollution. He is scathing about our attitude towards air pollution and pollution of the waterways and our lack of willingness to address this if it involves any personal cost. The individual consumer doesn't want the real cost of disposing of leftovers included in the price of his goods, and firms refuse to bear the cost of recycling or treating their waste products unless they are given tax relief. Private profit matters more than the public environment.[17]
- His fourth example is the foolish and total destructiveness of modern warfare.

We wonder what he would have to say 45 years later. Intriguingly he uses a metaphor of the West as a spoiled child scattering broken plastic toys around the room expecting that his two nursemaids, air and water, will clean up the mess. The reason we say it is intriguing is that Greta Thunberg used the same metaphor in a speech to the European Economic and Social Committee in 2019 entitled 'You're Acting Like Spoiled Irresponsible Children'.[18]

The current system is broken and we have so far failed to imagine a meaningful alternative. We need to learn to dream again.[19] We need a whole new way of thinking.[20] We need a new story, a new script to live by. Rowan Williams puts it like this: 'Change the narrative and who knows what is possible? Accept the diseased imagination of the culture we have created and the death count begins now. Anger, love and joy may seem like odd bedfellows but these are the seeds of a future that will offer life – not success but life.'[21]

At the same time as John Taylor's newsletter in 1972, the first world conference on the environment took place and the report 'Limits To Growth' was published. One of the authors, Donella Meadows, pulls back the curtain on the current system of so-called progress and growth without limits when she says 'Growth is one of the stupidest purposes ever invented by any culture ... We've got to have an enough.'[22]

Therein lies the heart of the matter. We have told ourselves a story of growth, of progress, of ever-rising prosperity and this is why the issue of economics is so closely related to the environment. Progress has turned out to be rather like the gods of the Old Testament who seem to offer so much but whose ways lead to death rather than life and who demand the sacrifice of children on their altars.

Where might we find an alternative imagination if our gods have failed us? Can we find an alternative way of 'an enough'?

An economics and theology of Enough

There are plenty of different ways to organize society, so it is rather odd that we have got so stuck in our current ways of operating. The word 'economics' in its Greek root relates to household management. Kate Raworth brilliantly reimagines economics for the twenty-first century by proposing a very different storyline. Taking the image of the household she says that the economic challenge is simply, 'to manage our planetary home in the interest of all its inhabitants'.[23] Rather than a degenerative economy that is addicted to growth and runs along the lines of take – make – use – lose, which draws on and drains earth's resources, she says we need regenerative economies that enable renewable energy in which resources can be used again and again. Rather than economies that concentrate resources in the hands of fewer and fewer people, which is a design failure, we should design distributive economies.[24] She designs a model in which the goal is human thriving, keeping below the limits to safeguard the planet's life systems and keeping above a limit whereby all peoples' needs can be provided for. It is exactly the kind of imagining we need. It is a sustainable economics of enough within which the planet is safe.

One of the ideas that has had plenty of air time is a poverty line. In Raworth's model, with a distributive economy everyone would live above the poverty line. However, one of the problems in the current story is not simply poverty – it's excess.

The disparity between the haves and have nots has never been greater. The World Council of Churches published a report in 2016 called 'The Greed Line', in which they say that 'the reverse side i.e. excessive wealth has to be dealt with'.[25] They explore what greed is and develop a series of measures and indicators that enable a 'greed line' to be drawn. This could be used by individuals or churches or applied to the economies of whole countries. Undergirding the notion of the Greed Line is the belief that life in all its fullness is something that is shared in community, not something acquired by individual accumulation. This again is a wonderfully imaginative piece of work.

Taylor's way of talking about this is through the language of enough. He challenges and questions the perceived wisdom of economic theory by suggesting that Western countries should accept a levelling off in their standard of living by slowing down growth, investment and consumption. He proposes that 'in order that others may have more, we must be content with comparatively less'.[26] This requires a change of both attitude and lifestyle. There are no easy answers, no magic bullet and no response that does not require some level of sacrificial living. Taylor's response to countering this 'unbridled excess' is to exhort people to live differently. Christian discipleship affords the possibility of just such a way of life. 'We need a thoughtful, convinced minority that will *live* in such a way as to challenge the cherished beliefs of the consumer society and defy its compulsions.'[27]

Taylor outlines 'a theology of Enough' which he exhorts us to live by. He finds a horror of excess expressed in the Old Testament:

Israel's watchmen are blind, all of them unaware.
They are all dumb dogs who cannot bark,
Stretched on the ground, dreaming, lovers of sleep,
Greedy dogs that can never have enough. (Isa. 56.10, 11)

He also finds that the concept of 'enough' is a theme woven through the Scriptures. God's mystical manna is an early example of this. God gives them as much as they can eat –

no asceticism or frugality here. 'But when they measured it with an omer, those who gathered much had nothing over, and those who gathered little had no shortage; they gathered as much as each of them needed' (Ex. 16.18). However, those who hoarded it discovered that it became infested with worms and stank. The people only needed enough; hoarding demonstrated a lack of trust and possibly greed. This idea of enough is also worked out in the laws that governed their lives in the early days of the kingdom. There was the law of gleaning where the farmer was not to be mean: 'When you reap the harvest of your land, you shall not reap to the very edges of your field, or gather the gleanings of your harvest; you shall leave them for the poor and for the alien: I am the Lord your God' (Lev. 23.22). They were not to go over the olive boughs a second time nor completely strip the vineyard clean. The reasons are that there is something for the poor and to remind them of their own dependence on God.

There was the law of limited cropping. The soil was not to be exploited and every seventh year the land was to lie fallow. The crops, olive groves and vineyards were to be left unpruned to provide for those who had not been able to put anything aside. There was not only the injunction concerning every seventh year but also a Jubilee year, 'And you shall hallow the fiftieth year and you shall proclaim liberty throughout the land to all its inhabitants. It shall be a jubilee for you: you shall return, every one of you, to your property and every one of you to your family' (Lev. 25.10). This is a limit on excess in the system, a redistribution, a reboot, a greed line if you will.

The law of the first fruits was a check on unbridled excess. The first reaping, the first bottling, the firstborn animals and even the firstborn son were set aside for God. This was a humbling reminder of the people's dependence on God. 'So now I bring the first of the fruit of the ground that you, O Lord, have given me' (Deut. 26.10). The context of all this life under the old covenant was the sacrificial system and the creation story, where humanity was to act as God's representative and steward in the world. We were given dominion, not domination. Taylor foresaw the awful consequences of turning dominion into domination. 'When man rejects his responsible sonship he turns into the anxiously assertive spoiled child who must at all costs have his own way. His God-given dominion becomes raving domination. Technology is safe only in a context of worship. Science should walk hand in hand with sacrifice.'[28]

Taylor calls the Old Testament community the 'Kingdom of Right Relationships' which embodied a theology of Enough. Creditors must exercise restraint, all loans must be interest-free, and every seventh year all loans were forgiven. 'Every seventh year you shall grant a remission of debts' (Deut. 15.1). Slavery was still accepted but every seventh year slaves were offered their freedom (Deut. 15.12).

The law of tithing was another law to glorify God and to counter selfish excess but it also had a surprising side, expressed in extravagant celebration:

Set apart a tithe of all the yield of your seed that is brought in yearly from the field. In the presence of the Lord your God, in the place that he will choose as a dwelling for his name, you shall eat the tithe of your grain, your wine, and your oil, as well as the firstlings of your herd and flock, so that you may learn to fear the Lord your God always. But if, when the Lord your God has blessed you, the distance is so great that you are unable to transport it, because the place where the Lord your God will choose to set his name is too far away from you, then you may turn it into money. With the money secure in hand, go to the place that the Lord your God will choose; spend the money for whatever you wish – oxen, sheep, wine, strong drink, or whatever you desire. And you shall eat there in the presence of the Lord your God, you and your household rejoicing together. As for the Levites resident in your towns, do not neglect them, because they have no allotment or inheritance with you. (Deut. 14.22–27)

This was a lavish and extravagant party expressing joy, generosity and plenty. It would be easy with the language of enough to adopt a mindset of scarcity but God is generous and abundant. This was powerfully and completely opposed to greed, exploitation, hoarding and turning everything back into profit. This generosity is also to be expressed towards those who are less fortunate:

> Every third year you shall bring out the full tithe of your produce for that year, and store it within your towns; the Levites, because they have no allotment or inheritance with you, as well as the resident aliens, the orphans, and the widows in your towns, may come and eat their fill so that the Lord your God may bless you in all the work that you undertake. (Deut. 14.28, 29)

In our historic past, public holidays were religious and were feast days. Every great house offered their hospitality to the poor and the less well off as part of the feast. Excess is not forbidden but there is a generous hospitality of give and take. In the New Testament these generosities are extended to all people, not just the Israelites. 'They are no longer an expression of family or tribal or religious solidarity.'[29] There is the same emphasis on resisting excessive wealth and greed. Taylor insists that the word we have often translated as covetousness (*pleonexia*) 'does in fact mean "excess" or "wanting more and more"'.[30] His outworking of Enough is not a grim or regimented rule designed to remove all joy from life, but rather a liberating trust in God to provide and an acknowledgement that celebrating and joy are an important part of what it means to be human.

No one is too small to make a difference

It is not enough just to say or believe these things, 'we have to opt out of the drift and help one another to live in cheerful protest against it'.[31] Or as Greta Thunberg puts it a bit more directly, 'I want you to act as if our house is on fire because it is.'[32]

There are two easy responses to the crisis we face. One is thinking that in order to make any significant difference change has to be at the level of international law and government policy and anything we do personally is simply a drop in the ocean, and this can lead to a sort of fatalism and inaction. Harry and Chris helpfully make the point that the ocean is made of drops in their song called 'Drop in the ocean', so that small actions are crucial:

> They say it's just a drop in the ocean
> As if that's a reason to stop
> But maybe they've forgotten the ocean
> Is literally made up of drops.[33]

The other easy response is to despair of any wider change and simply focus on the personal. The scale of change we need requires action on both fronts.

John Taylor would have loved Greta Thunberg! She is a remarkable person, aged 16 at the time of writing, who has sought to engage in both wider and personal change together. In 2018 she decided not to go to school but to protest outside the Swedish parliament for the sake of the climate. That sparked a global movement inspiring millions of pupils worldwide to join her in action against the climate crisis. Her first book, with the title *No One is Too Small to Make a Difference*, is a collection of her speeches and is short, direct and accessible. Somehow we need to keep alive that spirit and attitude of both the personal and political wherever we can.

We have found that a helpful framework for thinking about discipleship in today's world is through a threefold consideration of soil, soul and society.[34] Alastair Macintosh, who develops this in his book *Rekindling Community*, describes it as the triune basis for community. The risk here, in this section of this book, is that it becomes a list of things to do that could be either guilt inducing or limiting. Rather, we hope that it will spark our imagining about how we might live. The particular things we suggest may or may not grab you, but we hope you might be inspired to explore for yourself or with a group the questions of how you might become better lovers of the earth, of God, and of the community and develop a theology and spirituality rooted in the earth and land that can be lived out joyfully and faithfully.

Soil

We began this chapter by telling the story of salvation as a story of God's world. Soil is about connection and community with the land, the earth itself. We are all too easily disconnected from the land. Our first challenge is to become lovers of the earth, the land, the home in which we live. That can be nurtured in multiple ways. The first and simplest is to pay attention to it and appreciate the beauty of the world around us. Find a piece of land that you can look after and care for. That might be a garden, a woodland, an allotment. Maybe there is a piece of land owned by a local church? Join as a volunteer with something like the National Trust. There are increasing numbers of community co-operatives related to woodland and common land, community gardens and allotments. In many ways it is more fun to do it with a group and is a great way to build community. Get outside! Walk, run, swim, cycle. Look at and learn the names of trees in your street and neighbourhood. Jonny recently realized that he had been walking down his street for 20 years and didn't know the names of the trees lining it, so he has sought to find out what they are and get to know them. Get curious about plants and birds and clouds and insects. If you have children in your wider family involve them in nature. Evoke your own and their sense of wonder. Make compost – it's like magic – your food waste becoming rich soil that you can add to the land you look after. As a rule of thumb, try and put back into the soil as much as you take out.

As you engage in the outdoors and the natural world you will find that you start to have questions and become curious and learn more. It is great to learn more about God's beautiful world and its cycles of life and growth and renewal. Through that you learn how to look after things better. One of the things

Jonny has learned through that curiosity is just how amazing trees are, how creaturely, how social. He has learned how to create a richer ecosystem through a diverse culture rather than a monoculture. He has learned about wilding and rewilding. He has learned how to grow his own food. He has learned about diseases. He has learned that some of our methods of farming are much better than others for the earth.

In relation to the planet's warming we need to stop taking fossil fuel out of the ground and to develop renewable energy. At the personal level we can switch our supplier to a provider that uses green energy, we can share lifts, use public transport, fly as little as possible, holiday closer to home, reduce the use of plastic as much as we can, insulate our homes, eat less (or no) meat, pick up litter. At the political level, we can lean on our local councils to develop policy, provide electric charging points, start local energy companies rather than relying on the big fossil fuel providers. The other solution to global warming is to find a way to take carbon out of the atmosphere. It is foolhardy to rest our hopes on technology to get us out of the mess to which in many ways technologies have contributed. But we do know that one of the best ways to take carbon out of the atmosphere is trees. Trees are incredible. Plant trees, join campaigns to get trees planted. If you do have to fly, then offset your carbon by investing in tree planting. We need millions of trees planted in the UK and in the world. Where could you get involved in tree planting locally or globally?

Land and land ownership is a political issue everywhere and that is as true in the UK as anywhere. Land ownership needs new imagination, policies, distribution, to create limits on the accumulation of land by a few powerful elites and to create more commons. We have seen protests growing as people believe governments are not doing what needs to be done and pressure needs to be applied. Jonny has joined Extinction Rebellion and is a member of Greenpeace as he wants to join and collaborate with others who are lovers of the earth.

Soul

Soul is about connection and community with God, God's Spirit, and a developing awareness of self in relation to God and God's world. Far too often our spirituality is otherworldly and super spiritual, singing about God on high, in the heavens, about intimacy with God with our eyes closed. How might we reconnect it to this world with our eyes open? We need new liturgies, prayers, songs, theologies, and rituals that articulate connection with the soil. We should lament with sorrow the loss of species and the planet's warming, and pray and work for its healing and renewal. How can the cycle of the Church's year connect with the rhythms of creation's seasons? What is a spirituality of enough?

To give an example of how this might be incorporated in worship, the community Jonny is part of, Grace, had a worship service in which there was a station on the theme of soil. On the floor was a layer of soil and people were invited to take a moment to be still and place their hands in the dirt with these words of reflection:

You are human, made in God's image
Adam was the first human – the word adam means 'of the soil'
You are made from dirt, from soil, from the stuff of
    the earth
We are earthy
Place your hands in the soil and be still
Feel the groan of the earth in our times and pray
Feel the joy of the earth in all its beauty and give thanks
And be still.

The word 'soil' was spelled out in candles in the soil and by way of lament for our role in the heating of the earth, people were invited to blow out a candle, pray for the earth's cooling and to confess our corporate sin against the earth. There were also stations reflecting on waste with compost that people could add to; another with water and paper drops that people could write small actions on which they could commit to as their 'drops in the ocean', inspired by the Harry and Chris song above.[35]

In the Church, care for creation is one of the Five Marks of Mission.[36] Perhaps that is the one that should be at the front and centre of mission in the decades to come, without losing the heart of mission which is Jesus Christ? It would be wonderful to think that anyone who was concerned with the earth would immediately think of the Church as a community that cares for the earth, where they would find a soulful spirituality in which to be at home. Being a disciple of Jesus Christ is to discern where God is at work and join in, using the gifts and the person that we are, made in God's image. Part of our soul-work is to become more fully ourselves as we seek to join in creation's healing.

Society

Society is connection to community both locally and in the wider human community on planet earth. John Taylor suggests that a good place to start is with whoever is at home. He encourages families to live a life that is simple, based on the principles of Enough and not on the principles of a 'more and more' ethos. These should be practised with a sense of fun rather than with an earnest, dogged determination that removes any sense of joy and pleasure and risks forgetting that God is a God of grace. Some of his suggestions are as follows:

- limit your family to one child of your own and one adopted brother or sister
- buy unadvertised brands
- no second helpings unless there are guests
- no second car and perhaps not even one – we might add join a car share, use public transport, go electric
- go for quality products that will last
- go for the new-style hospitality: simple fare and a much wider circle of guests
- develop the hospitality of our car also.[37]

These ideas may somewhat reflect the 1970s, but they present us with the challenge of continuity and contextualization for the twenty-first century.

The power of consumer culture is so all-pervasive that it can be really hard to do something on your own. So as well as in the home, little congregations as outlined in Chapter 1 or mission communities and home groups are great spaces in which to explore how to live together with enough. There is real richness and practical wisdom in the monastic and other Christian traditions that have lived in community; they have some well-proven insights to contribute that will strengthen the movement as a whole.[38] We can learn from communities such as Lee Abbey and Scargill, the Iona Community and the Taizé Community what these new forms have to offer. Of course, they are not essential to defying our consumerist society but 'these outposts of an alternative life-style are very important to the Christian resistance movement'.[39]

Taylor gives examples from a range of contexts. He cites a short-term experiment in group living in a redundant Bedfordshire church, a small community of three Roman Catholic monks, the Christian ashram movement, and the Dilaram House movement (Houses of the Peaceful Heart) – a community that began in Nepal and reached out to young travellers. He commends the CMS system of financial support for mission partners, 'sufficient for life and health but not for luxury or saving', and wonders if that model could not be adopted as a basis for 'a voluntary sharing of resources to provide a common basic income and a margin for the work of the kingdom'.[40] Housing has become a really big issue – home ownership is simply not an option for young people in the way that it was and we require new imagination for housing models.

These principles can also be applied to churches. How do we spend our money? On ourselves and building projects, or can we be generous with our gifts to those in the world church who may be more in need? This will mean some sacrificial giving and letting go of some of our own dreams and projects.

Let us try to lighten the institutional machinery of our Church and recover the sense of the provisional and the spirit of poverty which is so free and so strong. Let us stop trying to keep up with the Jones's in expensive apparatus and techniques, and go for simplicity of means in our mission.[41]

This is a clarion call to simplicity of structures, governance and lifestyle within our churches.

Along with economist Dr Francis Schumacher, best known for his work *Small is Beautiful, A Study of Economics as if People Mattered*, Taylor promotes the value of people over profit in technology, aid and economic theory.[42] He gives examples from East Africa, where profits and sophisticated technology are prioritized over local needs and context. A textile factory in East Africa was so highly automated that it needed only 500 workers and yet the government had asked for the factory to be built in this particular region because of high unemployment. Armed guards were placed at the gates of the factory to keep out the crowds of young Africans who were desperate for jobs. Technology has now developed robots and AI so that this issue has escalated. For Taylor, the rationale for Enough is found in Schumacher's book title – people. Not goods but people. Not profits but people. Not even efficiency but people. This goes back to Kate Raworth's economics, in which the goal is human flourishing rather than growth and profit at any cost.

The wider international human community is ultimately our society, our community, made in God's image. The impact of global warming on the planet will test international relations as areas of land become uninhabitable and there are huge migrations because of climate change. How will we show welcome and hospitality? The Church is one of the most amazing global networks and she will need to lead the way in compassion, advocacy and solidarity as we seek to share our home and live with enough. Taylor suggests that the question each of us has to ask, time after time, is this: 'Will this purchase, this change, these plans, make our relationships more fully human in the context of our own one human family? Will this enrich or impoverish the personal value of other people? Will it clarify or cloud man's [sic] recognition of himself as the child of God?'[43]

Exercising Creativity

Idea + Work

We love people who come up with ideas that solve problems that then become reality. This is especially impressive when in order to solve a particular problem you actually have to reimagine the world, because the paradigm itself is part of the problem. Pete Dearman is one example.[44] He invented an engine that emits zero carbon. He initially began by messing around with his lawnmower and antifreeze. As an engineer he figured that what drives a piston is temperature change and you could drive a piston by moving the temperature from sub-zero to zero if you used liquid nitrogen along with isothermal expansion. He has invented an engine that is not oil dependent and has a by-product of refrigeration which is brilliant in hot climates with a lot of food wastage. This last year he has just negotiated two big contracts with China. His story is one of many of outsiders rebooting our world by having to reimagine the way the world is organized in order to come up with a solution to the problem.[45]

There are two stages to creative thinking – the idea and the work. Our reflections so far have focused on the first. According to Phil Beadle that is the easy part, but the more important part is the process of construction that requires effort, discipline, grind and putting in the hours.[46] We often use 'dreamers who do' as a description for pioneers because it brings together the dreaming and the work.[47] Grayson Perry says that when asked for the one tip he would give to art students he replies, 'Turn

up on time, be nice and put in the hours.'[48] Austin Kleon
has a section in his book for artists entitled 'Be Boring'
which includes timekeeping, money, and life issues.[49] The
Do Lectures have produced two brilliant reports aimed
at creatives – the *Side Project Report* and *The Stress
Report*, in which they address issues of time, resourcing,
resilience, support, team, looking after yourself, failure,
what to do when you go through the dark forest or wilderness and so on.[50] You get the point – design thinking and
innovation has more to it than ideas and imagination.
Those are crucial, but being aware of further stages in
the process of innovation is also essential.

In most cases, innovation begins with dissatisfaction,
anger, frustration or grief. There is something bugging a
person that leads them to wonder about solutions, how
things could be different. It is here that ideation kicks in.
If anger or dissatisfaction is one side of motivation then
passion is the flipside of this and together they create
drive and energy for change.

Then there is a phase of exploration, trial and error,
experimenting and learning in an iterative process and
changing the design or idea accordingly. This no doubt
involves action and testing prototypes. James Dyson
famously got through over 5,000 prototypes on the way to
creating the Dyson vacuum cleaner.

Mike Moynagh describes a third phase: the emergence
of 'sense making' as the design unfolds. The process is
dynamic and you have to respond to how it develops and
what emerges, making sense of it as you go.[51] These three
stages together are a kind of feeling your way. In the business world, and often in the church world, people like to
know exactly where you are going and what the outcomes
will be. This simply doesn't work in this sort of innovation,
which requires much more risk and experimentation. We
found the description of this process of innovation really
helpful because we realized that this uncertain adaptive

and flexible approach was normal rather than vague or woolly, which it can look to those in more stable and fixed worlds.

Once a prototype has been designed and tested it can then be amplified or scaled up and lead towards wider transformation. The Dearman engine has now reached this exciting stage. It is also an entirely normal part of the process on the journey to the new to find yourself in the wilderness or a dark forest, facing disbelief, opposition or the money running out and wondering if and how you will ever get to the new place. Resilience, looking after yourself, having friends and support are a crucial part of the journey.

At all stages there is the question of resourcing, both in time and money, and persuading others to back an idea. There are various models and approaches to resourcing. Depending on the scale of project, one that is really worth considering is the idea of a side project. That is the way we have started lots of projects. The big plus is that they don't have to bear the burden of putting bread on the table – they can run alongside other things. The challenge with side projects, of course, is time and it needs determination to focus on doing what needs doing. A key resource is other people. Who might get involved with you in a team? Are there people you can collaborate with? As a side project grows it can then shift to becoming the main thing. The pioneer training at CMS grew like this. It began as a series of one-off evenings and days. It then expanded to a series of weekends and then became a university accredited course. At each stage the resourcing required and the business model had to change.

And all of this requires work and determination!

In the face of environmental crisis and the culture of global excess and inequality, the kind of imagination we need is prophetic. Prophets evoke grief for the way things are because tears will break the numbness people experience in the face of the dominant culture. They also create amazement and energize hope that new worlds are possible when that seems impossible.[52] That hope needs to be embodied and enacted by dreamers who do, by those who can give ideas legs by combining the two phases of creativity – the idea and the work.

Exercises

1   What are you dissatisfied with? What is frustrating you? What are you angry about in the world? Express grief for that issue either through a poem or piece of art or by creating a way to ritualize that loss with a community to which you belong. Where in the tradition of the Gospel is there something that speaks to this issue? How might you draw on that alternative imagination in the present? Take that same issue or concern and imagine a future where it is no longer an issue. What can you do in the present to lead towards that different future? Come up with a list of 'drops in the ocean' and pick one or two that you can do now.

2   Take the three areas of soil, soul and society. What is a practice that you could engage with in each of these three areas?

3   Do you have an idea for a side project? If so, what is the next step you could take to move it forward? Who else might join with you in that adventure?

Notes

1 Richard Middleton, *A New Heaven and a New Earth* (Grand Rapids: Baker Academic, 2014), p. 39.

2 *CMS Newsletter*, No. 363, September 1972.

3 Romans 8.21–22.

4 Hans Küng, *On Being a Christian* (New York, NY: Doubleday, 1974).

5 For a discussion of this in relation to hymnology, see Tom Wright, *Surprised by Hope* (London: SPCK, 2007).

6 Athena Peralta and Rogate Mshana, *The Greed Line* (Geneva: World Council of Churches, 2016), p. 3.

7 William Ripple and Nicholas Houtman, 'Scientists' Warnings Have Been Ignored', in Extinction Rebellion, *This is Not a Drill* (London: Penguin Random House, 2019), p. 30.

8 Ripple and Houtman, 'Scientists' Warnings', p. 30.

9 Rachel Carson, *Silent Spring* (London: Houghton Miffin, 1962).

10 www.ipcc.ch.

11 David Wallace Wells, *The Uninhabitable Earth* (London: Penguin Books, 2019), p. 3.

12 Wells, *The Uninhabitable Earth*, p. 138.

13 *CMS Newsletter*, No. 363, September 1972.

14 John Taylor, *Enough is Enough* (London: SCM Press, 1975).

15 *CMS Newsletter*, No. 363, September 1972.

16 *CMS Newsletter*, No. 363.

17 *CMS Newsletter*, No. 363.

18 Greta Thunberg, *No One is Too Small to Make a Difference* (London: Penguin Random House, 2019), p. 34.

19 Thunberg, *No One is Too Small*, p. 13.

20 Thunberg, *No One is Too Small*, p. 36.

21 Rowan Williams, 'Afterword', in *This is Not a Drill*, p. 184.

22 Donella Meadows in Kate Raworth, *Doughnut Economics* (London: Random House Business Books, 2017), p. 40.

23 Kate Raworth, 'A New Economics' in *This is Not a Drill*, p. 146.

24 Kate Raworth, *Doughnut Economics*, p. 163.

25 Peralta and Mshana, *The Greed Line*, p. 5.

26 *CMS Newsletter*, No. 363, September 1972.

27 *CMS Newsletter*, No. 363.

28 *CMS Newsletter*, No. 363.

29 *CMS Newsletter*, No. 363.

30 *CMS Newsletter*, No. 363. See Frederick William Danker, *A Greek-English Lexicon of the New Testament and other Early Christian Literature*, third edition BDAG (Chicago: University of Chicago Press,

2000–2), p. 824. Πλεονεξία (*pleonexia*), the state of desiring to have more than one's due, greediness, insatiableness, avarice, coveoutness.

31 *CMS Newsletter*, No. 363.

32 Thunberg, *No One is Too Small*, p. 24.

33 'Drop in the Ocean' by Harry and Chris, used with permission.

34 Alastair Macintosh, *Rekindling Community* (Totnes: Green Books Ltd, 2008).

35 This service outline, with photos, is available here: https://jonny baker.blogs.com/jonnybaker/2020/01/soil-soul-society.html.

36 See www.anglicancommunion.org/mission/marks-of-mission.aspx.

37 *CMS Newsletter*, No. 383, July 1974.

38 *CMS Newsletter*, No. 383.

39 *CMS Newsletter*, No. 383.

40 *CMS Newsletter*, No. 383.

41 *CMS Newsletter*, No. 363, September 1972.

42 See F. Schumacher, *Small is Beautiful, A Study of Economics as if People Mattered* (London: Blond and Briggs, 1973). The *Times Literary Supplement* ranked *Small Is Beautiful* among the 100 most influential books published since World War Two. See www.goodreads.com/list/show/38381.TLS_The_Hundred_Most_Influential_Books_Since_the_Second_World_War (accessed 28.3.2019).

43 *CMS Newsletter*, No. 363, September 1972.

44 His story is told in Mark Stevenson, *We Do Things Differently* (London: Profile Books, 2017), p. 100.

45 *We Do Things Differently* is full of such stories.

46 Phil Beadle, *Rules for Mavericks* (Carmarthen: Crown House Publishing, 2017), p. 84.

47 Gerald Arbuckle, *Refounding the Church: Dissent for Leadership* (London: Geoffrey Chapman, 1993), p. 7.

48 Grayson Perry, in Bob and Roberta Smith and Edmund de Waal et al, *The Creative Stance* (London: Common Editions, 2016), p. 14.

49 Austin Kleon, *Steal Like an Artist* (New York: Workman Publishing, 2012), p. 116.

50 David Hieatt, *The Side Project Report* (London: The Do Lectures, 2015) and *The Stress Report* (London: The Do Lectures, 2016).

51 Michael Moynagh, *Church in Life* (London: SCM Press, 2017), pp. 28–36 explores six stages of emergence in innovation which I draw on here, one of which is sense making.

52 Walter Brueggemann, *The Prophetic Imagination* (Minneapolis, MN: Fortress Press, 1978), says that evoking grief and energizing hope are the two tasks of the prophet.

6

The Yeast of Nonconformity

There are only religious *people*

We are living in a context of increasing religious diversity and, to the surprise of many Western commentators, the world is becoming increasingly religious. 'In 2020 the vast majority of people worldwide – 88.7 per cent – profess to adhere to a religion.'[1] Asia is the most religiously diverse continent. However, migration means that religious diversity is increasing elsewhere, with some of the most profound increases found in Germany and the USA. In an era where religious beliefs and even religious diversity can be weaponized and where the media can portray difference and otherness as something to be feared, we need to learn how to engage with people of other faiths and how to listen to and learn from them. We think that the first step is to engage with people rather than the concepts. It is important to study and learn about other faiths, to discover not only their goodness and beauty but also their differences. However, ultimately it is actual encounter with people of other faiths that matters. Barbara Brown Taylor reminds us in her book, *Holy Envy*, that there is no such thing as '*religion*, there are only religious *people*, who embody the scripts of their faiths as differently as dancers embody the steps of their dances'.[2] This is vital to remember. There is no such thing as a generic Buddhist or Muslim – or Christian for that matter. When you have met one Muslim, you have met one Muslim. When you have met one Christian, you have met one Christian. This applies to all faiths. We may all agree on aspects of our own religious teachings, but our experience and our living out of them will be plural and multifaceted, not singular and monochrome. Moreover, Brown Taylor asserts that this is 'as true within our religions as it is between them'.[3]

John Taylor was a keen student of the people and the thought systems of other faiths. He was interested in what we, as Christians, could learn from them and how we could relate to them more openly. As General Secretary of a mission agency that had mission partners in countries where Christianity was a minority faith, he wanted to observe and learn how to relate to people of other world faiths. His regular visits to the Middle East, Asia, West and East Africa all helped him to reflect more deeply on this.

He believed that the only way was costly and unconditional friendship. Mutual trust and companionship are needed so that irreconcilable differences can become topics for discussion and learning, rather than battlegrounds of conflict. This is not an easy road but Taylor believed that this was the way forward when relating with those of other faiths. Christian witness must be alongside as companions in a context of trust and respect, and not over and against those of another faith. We must also have the courage to listen to and to learn what other faiths know of Jesus. This is a risky and costly path and can only be forged through deep friendship and exchange of ideas which, traditionally, has been expressed through dialogue.

Dialogue as exchange and dangerous openness

Taylor framed dialogue firmly within this context of friendship and relationship. He sharply criticized its use as a technical and academic term, where scholars sit around tables giving their prepared speeches with little passion or enthusiasm. He much preferred the term 'exchange' as he believed that this could operate at many different levels, sometimes unplanned and unconsciously. Moreover, it is always mutual and normally happens within the context of friendship. He challenged his readers and asked how many of them are actually making friends with people from other faiths. He critiqued our lack of engagement: 'the fault in our mission today is not an aggressive proselytism but an almost total lack of human friendship across the religious and ideological frontiers. The Church is still living within her own Christendom long after that Christendom ceased to be western.'[4]

This is still a challenge to us today. How many of us have friends from other faiths and have shared lives together? There are examples of churches and groups around the country trying to engage and a good way to do this is through hospitality and food. Here is one example from The Table in the diverse multi-faith community of Southall, London; an area with 94 per cent ethnic diversity. The Table was launched as a Fresh Expression congregation of St John's Southall in 2017. It is important to note that this developed after ten years of connecting with the local community and building firm friendships. The intention was to be multicultural, reflecting the neighbourhood, and to be firmly Jesus-centred. It is a space where all people are welcome to creatively explore and experience knowing God. They meet monthly around a meal and worship. Those who attend are from a wide range of communities: Christian, Sikh, Muslim, Hindu, South-Asian, Iranian, African, Caucasian, asylum-seekers and migrants. People attend because they are made to feel welcome, they are free to bring their gifts, so that there is a sense of mutual sharing and reciprocity, and often the guests can become hosts, which points to an intriguing reversal of roles.

Ethnically diverse areas such as Southall have emerged because of our history of migration. One in five Europeans migrated between 1800 and 1925, the largest migration movement in history. This period also coincided with the high tide of the Western missionary movement as well as Empire. These movements unleashed powerful forces of change which have been reacting on Europe and England, in particular, ever since. For example, at the height of British colonial rule, the Queen of England had more Muslim subjects than any other ruler. This meant that England was open to Muslim and other immigration and settlement from the late nineteenth century. This sharp rise in immigration is a good example of one of these powerful forces at work, as people from former colonies or countries with which England had political or trade links found their way to the country. The religious implications and complexities of this are huge, as we are all beginning to realize. The migrants from the Majority World are generally religiously devout. They challenge our secularized outlook, our understanding of the supernatural, our understanding of liberal democracy and what it means to live together on these small islands.

Idina Dunmore, who leads The Table, offers a fascinating insight into what we can learn from migrants and those of other faiths. Citing 'the blessed reflex' where Christians from the Majority World are reviving Christianity in the West by their vibrant and passionate faith, she applies this to a multi-faith context. Dunmore claims that this blessed reflex comes not only from Christian migrants,

> but also from those of other religions, because encounter with other faiths and interfaith engagement can be a *means of grace* by which the Christian disciple is renewed and encouraged in her own faith and the Church can recover its vocation.[5]

Dunmore sees this as an example of dialogical hospitality and what Taylor might call a 'dangerous openness'. Taylor's example of this dangerous openness is instructive. He suggested that in our openness to learn from other faiths, new things may emerge. Might this not be syncretism? Perhaps, but it depends on how risky we are willing to be and on how much trust we have in the Holy Spirit. Taylor cited a fascinating example of village Christians in Andhra Pradesh in India, where it was observed that both the Christian and the Hindu communities influenced one another. The outcome was revealing with respect to witness and interest in the Gospel.

> Because the Christians have such a low wall of protective Christian culture around them, Hindu influence easily penetrates the Christian community, but the same absence of a pro-

tective wall makes it relatively easy for the Christian Gospel to be conveyed to a non-Christian. Crisis and opportunity are both present in the Christian's involvement in village life, and we may well ask, whether this is not more than a sociological fact, whether it is not an indication of the way God deals with his Church.[6]

When there was not the same 'dangerous openness' the mutual flow dried up. 'It is curious but perhaps finally quite understandable, that in this village, where the Christians have gone the furthest in developing a distinctively Christian community, there is the least interest in the Gospel on the part of the Hindus.'[7] It seemed that Christian distinctiveness and a desire to protect the community from Hindu influence was actually counter-productive to witnessing to the Gospel. Taylor is also hinting here that there is a two-way flow, that both faiths have something to offer the other.

In the Indian context, Taylor was convinced that dialogue just happens. It does not have to be planned; it happens because we are friends and neighbours and we are interested in one another's lives. He was convinced that the authorities' suspicion of foreign missionaries in India was not because of their contact with Hindus but rather from their lack of it! How involved are we in the various contexts around us and how willing are we to exhibit that same dangerous openness to engage with the different and to learn new things for the sake of the Gospel?

For Taylor the essence of dialogue is a journey of exploration to discover the relevance of Jesus and to discover more of his fullness. Taylor believed that, 'a different *kind* of truth is demanded in different cultures and at different times'.[8] He pondered how what we call 'scientific truth' could be appropriated by Hindu or Confucian minds and therefore how the universal truth of Christ is understood and realized in different contexts. He suggested that those early disciples such as Paul, Apollos and John were freed from bondage to their particular Jewish or Greek worldview. They were than able to see their heritage as both judged and fulfilled by Christ. Taylor believed that the same dynamics are at play in dialogue. 'So, precisely because of our adoring conviction that Jesus is universal and unique, we cannot reduce our faith in him to one traditional philosophical or sociological form.'[9] However, the relevance of Jesus to another worldview cannot be recognized from the standpoint of our own. Therefore we enter into dialogue humbly, not only with an expectant and reverent curiosity but also with some dread and fear, for we are faced with otherness and difference which needs to be understood and accepted on its own terms. This is an otherness that cannot simply be assimilated into my own terms. As Anglican bishop and Islamic scholar, Kenneth Cragg, reminds us, 'Are we not faced with an otherness which cannot be reduced, abated, merged or interchanged?'[10]

Taylor recalls the Epiphany story and those 'mysterious representatives of other faiths' who found their way to the Christ child with their particular gifts. Subverting a common approach to this story he asserted that it was not in their great learning that they were wise, but rather in their question, 'Where is he?' This asking of questions, this search for Christ's relevance, is a dynamic form of dialogue rather than the more static approach of examining the propositions, doctrines, rituals and systems that make up a religious system. Of course the next Epiphany story is Jesus himself asking questions, modelling this approach of inquiry and exploration for us. It was in asking questions that the claim 'You are the Christ' was made, a discovery which Jesus himself enabled.

Dialogue is also a witness to Christ's love. Love affirms the things that are shared on the basis of our common, shared humanity. Dialogue will recognize commonalities of spiritual experience but will also uncover differences that are mutually exclusive. This may be painful but must be faced, as the missionary obligation of each faith is faced and encountered.

The uniqueness of Christ

Taylor acknowledged that we live in a pluralist society and that our temptation, when engaging with those of other faiths, is either to compromise the uniqueness of Christ or to turn in on ourselves and so adopt a ghetto mentality. This is why we need dialogue or exchange. Taylor relied heavily on the presence of the Holy Spirit to enable this dialogue. His understanding is that the Holy Spirit is uniquely present in Christ, and by extension the Church, and is universally present throughout the universe. This is a helpful distinction. Taylor likened the Holy Spirit to a 'fifth column in the heart of every man [sic]' calling us to respond.[11] This is what gave him the confidence that we can engage in dialogue – precisely because the Holy Spirit is active in both participants, although Taylor offers the caveat, 'on one side what he [the Holy Spirit] says is explicit and particular, while on the other it is more directional and responsive'.[12] Taylor believes that a religious system is a tradition of response to reality and that, as we engage in conversation with people of other faiths, we listen and learn so that we can begin to understand their view of reality. This is the only way we will understand how Christ meets and questions their needs, aspirations and dreams.

For Taylor, the Christian is absolutely convinced of the uniqueness and universality of Christ and is also confident 'that the Holy Spirit who has been at work through the centuries evoking the responses of that other Faith is ceaselessly pointing to Christ'.[13] Taylor does not see Christ as the fulfilment of every religion because Christ makes all things new. He insists on the newness and challenge that Jesus brings. Jesus challenges, completes and cleanses so that new wineskins are needed for the new wine.

He names Jesus as 'the great disturber'[14] who breaks into history and upsets traditions.

So if Christians are right in believing this Jesus to be the incarnation of the Word that has been universally at work from the beginning, then that Word, that eternal Son is to be discerned not so much in the orthodoxies of other faiths and ideologies, as in the yeast of the nonconformity and challenge which is always inherent in them. He is the Source of that stream of revival which flows through all religions by the grace of God. He is also to be found in the movement of history which compel men [sic] of faith to break old moulds and think new thoughts.[15]

Jesus is to be found in 'the yeast of nonconformity and challenge' in other faiths. This is indeed a startling way of thinking for those committed to a more static and unchanging view of Jesus and Christianity. Taylor is convinced that religions are systems made by humanity in which God's Spirit is active, constantly challenging and reforming. He believes that each religion 'is a long tradition of human response, both positive and negative, to the call of him who is beyond all religions'.[16] This tradition is then preserved by the faithful in each generation but is also occasionally disturbed 'by the vision and impatience of those who "hear" the Creative Word and bear witness, often opposed and persecuted by the upholders of orthodoxy'.[17] Taylor is challenging us to be far more risky and creative when we engage with those from other faiths, as well as within our own faith tradition, where we may have become stuck and unable to question our own traditions and shibboleths. We may wonder, who are the 'upholders of orthodoxy' in our generation? Where might we encounter 'the yeast of nonconformity and challenge'? Those of us who are in a secular context can ask ourselves this of secularization – what are the gifts of nonconformity that we can learn from it? While on a visit to New York, Taylor wrote that we must accept 'the secularities as the proper sphere of Mission because they are already the sphere of the Holy Spirit ... The new kind of evangelism means not looking at the world from inside the Church, but looking at the faith from inside the world.'[18] As we engage with people of other faiths and different ideologies, we need to be on the lookout for this, open to the challenge, gifts and renewal that they can offer us.

Taylor is firm that we must go with Christ into these new

worlds and not expect them to come to us. It is within their worlds that Christ will challenge, transform and revolutionize them.

> Either we must think of Christian mission in terms of bringing the Muslim, Hindu, the Animist into Christendom or we must go with Christ as he stands in the midst of Islam, of Hinduism, of the primal worldview, and watch with him, fearfully and wonderingly, as he becomes – dare we say it? – Muslim, or Hindu, or Animist, as once he became man and a Jew. Once, led by the Spirit, the Church made its choice in this matter at the Council of Jerusalem and dared to win Gentiles by becoming Gentile ... So Christ in his church answered the call of the Greeks – he came where they were and became what they were. From within their own culture he challenged their strength and judged their wisdom. He turned their world upside down just as he had turned Judaism upside down – just as, indeed, if he enters our churches today he turns our Christianity upside down. So would he challenge and judge and revolutionise the African worldview; but he must do it from the inside.[19]

This call to do this from the inside is radical, difficult and sacrificial because it demands a total identification and solidarity with the other. It is also a call to watch and wait with fear and trembling to discern just how this transformation will happen. Ultimately it is a call for the insider to be the missioner as the one on the inside is challenged, judged and turned upside down.

The *terra incognita* of Christ

Taylor engaged with the thinking of the German-Canadian Jesuit priest Klaus Klostermaier, who lived in India for some years, including in the sacred city of Vrindaban. For Klostermaier, dialogue that engages the deep things of the heart takes us beyond shallow certainties. Klostermaier claims that:

Our faith challenges us to risk our faith. As long as we are not ready to stake our own nearness to Christ for our brethren we do not know the meaning of faith. Unless we have reached the very bottom of our nothingness we do not know who Christ is.[20]

These are insights born out of years of living and breathing in another faith context. We resonate with the bold claim that 'Our faith challenges us to risk our faith.' We believe that our faith demands risk and vulnerability and the cross stands as an authentic sign of that vulnerability.

Taylor insisted that a missionary must be an explorer and an inquirer. He wrote, 'For what drives the true missionary of any race is not what he knows but what he doesn't know.'[21] For him, this is the essence of dialogue, which is a journey, an exploration, 'the long trek into the *terra incognita* of Christ'.[22] Much of Jesus' teaching about the kingdom is exactly this – not only about its hiddenness and its veiledness, but also about its unpredictability and the sheer length of time discovering it can take. Indeed, the journey into 'the *terra incognita* of Christ' can be a long, risky and even dangerous one.

Taylor reflected on the possibilities of shared worship and was influenced by Cragg's ideas on this, who believed that as we have so many shared concerns and struggles, why can we not voice these together. Taylor concurred with this but was concerned to acknowledge the uniqueness of Christ in worship as we are 'bound to grieve and inwardly protest when that Name is not confessed in the bowed knees of the man [sic] next to him'.[23] However, he reminded us that in the meantime we are in the 'already-not-yet' period, before Christ returns to reign:

The name that is above every name is hidden still, and Jesus, who never thought his equality with God a prize to grasp at, is humbler than his disciple. And the disciple can afford to keep his secret a little longer if, thereby, others are more likely to love his gentle Lord.[24]

The art of being a minority

In many of these multi-faith contexts that Taylor reflected on, there was a local church, usually small, vulnerable and sometimes fearful. He fully appreciated that links with the West often did not help their situation and were becoming increasingly an embarrassment, if not dangerous, for those in the local context. However, Taylor believed that this consequent vulnerability, smallness and sometimes even hiddenness were gifts that the Christian minority could offer to their context. 'Yet this very vulnerability of the Churches of the Middle East may open doors of communication with their non-Christian neighbours which have resisted the more confident hammering of the past.'[25] He was well aware that countries that had been under colonial rule or that had experienced colonialism as a negative influence may not respond positively to a gospel that seems to come from the outside or accompanied by foreign power and influence. We resonate with this and believe that this is even more accurate today, 60 years after he wrote this. Military might and power are still used by the West to impose their will on other countries.

We believe that the Gospel is shared most effectively within the everyday contexts in which Christian believers live and work. The Christian doctor, teacher, project manager, parent, will witness most effectively by being alongside their colleagues and doing their job or role as a Christian. The biblical model for this is to be salt and leaven, spread out in the community bearing the Gospel in this way. However, Taylor acknowledged that Islam, in particular, has traditionally walled Christians in and forced them to adopt a ghetto mentality. This can create an inward-focused perspective and an unhelpful defensiveness, even a fortress mentality among small Christian communities. Taylor believed that 'the Church must leap over the wall or perish'.[26] He gives examples of Christians working in cooperation with Muslim organizations fighting against sickness, poverty and injustice as the kind of Christian witness that is possible in these contexts. He quoted Kenneth Cragg who reminds us that 'minorities have to exist with their ultimate securities outside their own direct power and control'.[27] This is a very different context from one where a church is used to having status and power in society but it is a context that is more similar to that of the early church, increasingly so in our own day in Western societies. Arguably it is also closer to the way of Jesus, who clearly rejected the temptation of worldly power and lived on the margins of society. Christians need to learn how to practise the art of being a minority, being on the margins and on the edge. Richard Rohr writes about 'the edge of the inside'. He encourages this posture:

> When you live on the edge of anything with respect and honour, you are in a very auspicious and advantageous position. You are free of its central seductions, but also free to hear its core message in very new and creative ways.[28]

Stefan Paas, in his book *Pilgrims and Priests*, believes that the minority posture is the 'natural position' for Christians in the West, especially as we learn what it means to live as a Christian on other people's terms.[29]

Religious pluralism

Taylor believes that religious pluralism is a gift to us so that we may meet people of other faiths or of no faith. He believes that God is speaking to us through this enabling of an enlarged understanding of both God and humanity. He is quick to counter what he sees as three distortions in our response to pluralism:

1 The idea of the cosmic Christ or eternal Word present in all developments in human history. This idea can lead to Christ becoming merely an abstraction or a myth disconnected from the life of the church and real people today.
2 Christ as the Truth which fulfils all human aspirations in both the religious and secular realms. He believed that if

we overlook the Hebrew background to the story, we mis-
understand the nature of Christ's fulfilment. His was the
way of protest so he was put to death as a blasphemer and
a criminal. He fulfilled Judaism in the way of protest. For
Taylor, the gift of salvation comes 'only as an irruption, a
revolution, a new creation'.[30]

3 Since Christ is already Lord of all humanity, we do not
then need to strive to bring him to humanity. Taylor quotes
Klostermaier, who is scathing of this approach:

> They have an easy time, the 70° Fahrenheit theologians.
> They settle down in some library and find enough books
> there by means of which it can be proved that the
> non-Christian religions are the normal way to salvation
> for the non-Christian, that each one finds God even with-
> out mission, that one should not disturb the conscience of
> a non-Christian.[31]

Taylor clearly believed that we need to communicate the
uniqueness of Christ and not subscribe to a theology of
non-evangelism. He develops the idea of the mystery of the
pre-incarnate Christ to help us develop a doctrine of salvation
which could be beyond the Church, but not beyond Christ.
He asserted that our creeds have not made enough of this. We
have been shown, from the beginning, how our world was
held in existence by its Redeemer who was to die. For Taylor
this means that our being held in Christ is a more primary
condition than ignorance of Christ. 'Therefore, it follows that
any and every movement of his mind and spirit which can be
called an act of faith is truly faith in Christ, even though Christ
is still the unknown magnetic pole which draws him.'[32] He
was also insistent on the holistic and sometimes non-religious
nature of salvation. Jesus healed the paralytic and then talks
about forgiveness of sins; for the rich young ruler who wanted
a spiritual answer, Jesus gave him a lesson in economics. All
our human needs must be met, so for Jesus it does not seem to
matter much where he started. 'If faith can sometimes be faith
in a Christ who is not yet named, salvation does not always

need to be experienced in religious categories.'[33] This offers us
a fuller and richer understanding of salvation.

The Way of the Cross

Taylor proposed that the patterns of Gospel experience are in
fact the patterns of life itself. Jesus' life of freedom and protest,
his death and resurrection are both history and eternal reality.
They did happen and they are still the way things happen. We
ourselves are transformed by living out this pattern wherever
it emerges in our experience. However, our salvation is not
complete until we become a cross-bearer. We tend to think of
salvation as a liberation from suffering but Taylor suggests that
we are only fully human when we are bearing one another's
burdens. We can leave humanity's eternal destiny in the hands
of God; yet we yearn for humanity to walk 'consciously in the
steps and in the power of the Crucified'.[34] He was absolutely
insistent on the necessity and centrality of the cross – with all
its cost of suffering, silence and service. He cited this moving
story as an illustration:

> A missionary asked me in South India some time ago how I
> would have advised a Hindu woman who came to her con-
> fessing that she worshipped only Jesus and daily read the
> New Testament which she had secreted in the house. 'But,'
> she asked, 'must I be baptised? If I tell my husband even that
> I have such a desire he will turn me out. Our marriage will be
> broken, my children bereft of a mother, our family destroyed.
> Must I do that to them?' My every instinct demanded that I
> should say: 'No! This is not required.' When Jesus speaks
> of baptism, he means the cross: 'Are you able to be baptised
> with the baptism I am baptised with?'[35]

There is a costly price to be paid, in many contexts, for public
confession and baptism and Taylor did not shy away from
this. He quoted a Nepali pastor who poignantly told him, 'I
never baptise anyone until I know that he or she is able to

bear suffering.'[36] And yet he believed that, at a deeper level, all humanity shares a common, primeval world of longing and suffering and hope. So he explained that the cross is common ground, 'not our theological explanations of the cross but our recognition of it, our response to it, our experience of its desolation and of the mysterious resurrection which follows'.[37] He believes that this is the pattern of life that is worked out in various ways throughout history. Moreover, in order to be an effective witness we may need to be on the cross ourselves. It is in this very vulnerability and love, demonstrated on the cross, that Christian witness is at its most effective.

He gives a powerful example of this from the small and struggling church in Bangladesh, 'this One-Per-Cent Church',[38] which stood as an embodiment of sacrificial and hopeful love in a time of crisis. After a massive cyclone in 1970, the local clergy distributed relief supplies to Muslim and Christian alike, bridging the distrust between the Bengalis and the Biharis. Taylor observed that the ordinary church members, by sharing in the suffering alongside their Muslim neighbours and working together to meet the common need, emerged as more outward-looking and aware of the needs of the nation. This outworking of love points to the necessity to live and witness to the Gospel as a way of life. The CMS Asia Secretary at the time referred to this as 'a life quickened by the experience of the risen Lord'.[39] This way of life must be recognizable within and to the local context.

In the Indian context, Taylor insisted that the Church must allow herself to be more fully Indian 'because there is so much that is true and honourable, pure and lovely and of good report in India's thought and life, which can be found nowhere else'.[40] Christ is neither understood nor honoured if he is represented as an alien in a foreign tongue. He will not really be known in his fullness until he can be known and loved in the local context. Taylor makes a risky plea for the local culture to help the Church express this:

And because the church has been alienated for so long she may have to call upon the Hindu brother – the artist, musician or thinker – and trust his integrity to show her how to adore, and how to portray, her Lord in an Indian way.[41]

In his book, *The Primal Vision*, he posed a similar question, 'But if Christ were to appear as the answer to the questions that Africans were asking, what would he look like?'[42] What would Christ look like for Muslims, Hindus, Sikhs, Buddhists, pagans, those living on a particular housing estate, the local youth group, steam punks? This question is crucial for all contexts as disciples will not be able to follow the way of the cross if they do not know Jesus fully in their own heart language, culture and context.

An example of trying to imagine this in a small way comes from one of our students who rewrote a passage of Scripture to try to communicate The Word to Sikh culture. He explained that he wrote it in the style of the poetic verse of Sikh Scripture, the *Guru Granth Sahib*.

John 1.1–14

Always! Forever! The Word was.
The Word was with the Guru.
The Word was the Guru.
He sang the divine Music with the Formless One,
before the universes, worlds and continents were made.

World and Form were created by him,
All species and colours, Iron and fire.
No speck of dust exists except for him.

Where should men look for True Light?
In him who is True Life that is light for all.
Darkness and evil tries to extinguish the True Light,
Millions of times a day;
But the light beams out unfettered.

The Guru sent John. A holy saint.
He testifies about the True Light, ignoring caste.
He knew and saw and touched the True Light.

John was pure and devoted to God,
As a guru he brought light to men.
But he was not the True Light,
He pointed to the True One.

The True light that enlightens all men and all women,
Ignoring all caste and race,
Was entering into our existence.
He lived as the True Humble one.
The Maker of universes was universally unseen,
By the very eyes he had gifted sight to.
How could his own world never welcome him in?

Some holy people saw him.
Some put faith in his True Name.
They were reborn in God.
Born, not of gentle mother, strong father or family honour.
But reborn of, and for, God.

The True word became clay like us.
Spotless in moral character. Weak as we are.
Lived not in a palace, but worked alongside us.

What did he look like?
All the saints saw him,
Made manifest to us by the Father of all.
Radiant with Grace,
Resplendent with Holy Truth.[43]

The way of the cross is not the way of institutionalism. Taylor critiqued the Indian Church for this: 'The Indian church desperately needs to put off her institutionalism, for it is that which is western through and through.'[44] He asserted that the least important aspect of the Church is its power structures – its elections, committees, properties and statistics – for it is this that saps spirituality and true indigenization.

He abhorred the 'heartless way' in which Western powers forced their way into China in the nineteenth century and how Western nations used their technology and wealth to prove the superiority of the Gospel to a nation struggling to maintain its identity.

This has been a constant theme in the history of mission and we need to learn this lesson over and over again. Stefan Paas writes about this in the European context. He implores churches in the West to give up their historical (establishment?) privileges. He believes that only if we become weak will people be willing to listen.

> Only if people do not feel threatened by an institutional grasp for power by Christians will they feel free to appreciate what Christians have to tell. And only in this way will Christian communities have the room to develop a 'prophetic' alternative voice.[45]

He notes that in Amsterdam, as the churches have become numerically smaller and weaker, their influence throughout the city has increased as 'local government and other parties in society have warmed up to the churches'.[46] We need to recognize that the way of the Gospel is one of humility, vulnerability and weakness, just as the apostle Paul did (1 Cor. 2.1–5).

In the Middle-Eastern context, this plays out slightly differently. Taylor is sympathetic to the Muslim experience of fear and paranoia.

> To read modern history through Muslim eyes is to see a distorted image of relentless resolve on the part of Christian nations to dismember every effective Muslim power structure – first the Ottoman Empire, then the Emirates of West Africa, the united Arab resurgence, the Indonesian federation, Pakistan.[47]

In his opinion, the only way that this narrative of conquest and domination can be overcome is through love, perfect love. As Christians make friends with Muslims, they can engage in conversations of the heart. No law or surveillance can prevent this. CMS missionary Temple Gairdner was an Arabic scholar and author who spent most of his life in Egypt and loved the place and culture. He pleaded for this approach. 'We always need the *song* note in our message to the Muslims not the dry cracked note of disputation, but the song note of joyous witness, tender invitation.'[48] It is these qualities of love and tenderness that may be the most effective witness. We love this idea of the '*song* note' in our message – that our witness could be joyful and tender. This picks up Pope Francis' idea of a revolution of tenderness. Like John Taylor, he too has some wonderful word-pictures with respect to joyful witness:

> There are Christians whose lives seem like Lent without Easter. I realize of course that joy is not expressed the same way at all times in life, especially at moments of great difficulty. Joy adapts and changes, but it always endures, even as a flicker of light born of our personal certainty that, when everything is said and done, we are infinitely loved.[49]

Taylor's reflection on the church in Japan has a very different angle. He believed that it is exactly the uncompromising demands of Jesus that will speak to the Japanese soul and that they are willing to pay the price for a costly decision to follow Christ. 'In order to be indigenous to a culture the Church does not have to look for the points at which Jesus Christ is most easily acceptable, but rather at those points at which he most deeply challenges and saves.'[50] He quotes a theology lecturer from Kyoto who gives a number of creative experiments which are intentionally directed to break the Church out of its confinement and put it on the frontiers of industrial and urban life. He concluded his reflection on the church in Japan with this challenge from a woman who worked for the Textile Workers' Union:

> Abstract expressions are meaningless to listeners. What is necessary for effective witness by Christians is to be in the midst of all problems, struggling for solutions, making decisions. There may be a necessity to lead a wild-cat strike, to fight against the coercion of wrong authority. Such a need is often close to our existence in this present situation. Because

of our faith we may be forced to 'make our hands dirty' beyond popular ideas and ethics. If a Christian is hesitant about making a courageous decision under pressure and obstructions, the Christian faith may never put down its roots into the Japanese culture.[51]

This resonates with Paas's idea that when Christians have engaged with local government and society, their witness has been more effective.

Go with Christ

Taylor calls us to go with Christ in friendship and in humility into these worlds of other faiths, worlds with a dangerous openness. We are to witness to Christ with a bold humility, recognizing our own weakness and how much we still have to learn. Dialogue or conversation and exchange can teach all of us. Our own faith and life with Christ is nurtured and changed through these encounters and friendships. We hold firm to the uniqueness of Christ, but what an expansive kaleidoscope of colours and richness, what a subversion of values and traditions do we experience as we follow 'the great disturber' into these different contexts and faiths! This *terra incognita* is continually calling us on to new places, to terrifying places as we walk the way of the cross and bear one another's burdens. We know that following Christ can cost us everything, but may our witness be stirred with the yeast of nonconformity for the sake of the world for which Christ died.

Exercising Creativity

Provocations

In logical thinking your thoughts progress step by step in sequence, building from one thing to the next. This is an important way to think, but it rarely leads to new ideas. That's because the challenge in coming up with new ideas is to break from our usual pattern of thinking and get onto a different track. For that to happen we need to be interrupted or knocked off course. For example, imagine that one day there are roadworks blocking your regular route to work. To avoid the roadblock you take a side street and find to your surprise that it is more direct and takes some time off your journey. So that becomes your new route to work after the roadworks are completed. The only reason you discovered it was because of the roadblock that interrupted your routine. If you want to develop new ideas you should therefore welcome interruptions into your routine. A step on from that is to deliberately programme them into your routine so that you are regularly knocked off course. These interruptions are provocations.[52]

There are various kinds of provocations. Here are five suggestions of ones you could try, though there are of course lots of others. The most common is simply learning to receive what comes towards you and use it.[53] That might be something that is said or that you see, or something that happens to you. Brian Eno developed a set of cards called Oblique Strategies.[54] They are designed so that if you get stuck in the creative process you draw a card and have to receive that as a provocation. I am part of a photography group and we did an exhibition where each participant received a card at random and had to take a photograph in response to that.

A second kind of provocation is going in the opposite direction to the usual thinking pattern. Paul Arden's book

Whatever You Think Think the Opposite plays with this idea.[55] So, for example, one emerging church group, Ikon, ran an evangelism project where they invited other faiths to evangelize them rather than the other way round. This put them in the position of guests rather than hosts and gave them a genuine opportunity to listen and discover whether an encounter with other faiths might be a means of grace as Idina Dunmore suggests above.

A third kind of provocation is escape.[56] In this technique you imagine dropping something essential and play with this and see where it leads. So The Table has dropped language of church and describes itself as a Jesus-centred community. Perhaps its members have also exercised 'escape' by letting go of the usual Western understanding of conversion or membership and taking the risk of gathering round the table and building friendships to see where that leads.

One simple idea that is usually surprisingly effective is to take a random word and explore the connections with whatever it is you are reflecting on.[57] You can do this by simply using a dictionary or any book and landing your finger randomly on a word (or the nearest noun). It is important to go with the word you land on and not have another go to find something more palatable.

Art critic Lewis Hyde explores the character of Trickster in mythologies and the various ruses that Trickster comes up with in the stories.[58] One of those ruses is to mess with dirt. This is a fifth provocation. What is clean or dirty in a culture relates to the way society is ordered, so to mess with dirt is a challenge to the way society is ordered. Dirt is matter out of place.[59] So, for example, shoes on the table are dirty whereas by the door they are clean. Food on a plate is clean, food on the floor is dirt. Artists often use this method of provocation. The playful rewrite of John 1 above messes with what is sacred or pure (the Bible) by using language for God familiar to another culture to see what happens. This remakes the world in a way in which Christ seems to have come for Sikhs, which of course he has, and opens up the possibility of 'doing it from the inside' as John Taylor puts it. I remember the ripples of shock when a London youth worker created an Advent flyer with an image of a pregnant Mary wearing a hijab. I thought it was brilliant but it was a classic example of this trickster ruse.

If a provocation is genuinely provocative there is a temptation to judge it or resist it or defend against it. That tends to stop its potential in its tracks. One of the rules of improvisation in theatre is never to come against something, so if a comedy group is asking for suggestions for an improvisation, you will never hear them refuse a suggestion. Rather, they have learned that you get much more creative energy or movement from it by working with it and using that energy to swerve it in a different direction.[60] In some ways the more challenging or provocative the greater the potential.

Exercises

1 There are various provocations in this chapter. Here are two. Try receiving one and working with it to see where it leads you in your imagining:

- Jesus is to be found in 'the yeast of nonconformity and challenge' in other faiths.

- Either we must think of Christian mission in terms of bringing the Muslim, the Hindu, the Animist into Christendom, or we must go with Christ as he stands in the midst of Islam, of Hinduism, of the primal worldview, and watch with him, fearfully and wonderingly, as he becomes – dare we say it? – Muslim, or Hindu, or Animist, as once he became man and a Jew.

2 Try the random word provocation. Find a novel and pick a page at random and land your finger on a word (pick the nearest noun to that). Then explore this question using that word as a provocation: 'How might I make friends with someone from another faith?'

3 Try the 'escape' provocation as follows. Let go of church as a concept – that is your escape. Now imagine what mission with other faiths might look like without it. Where does that lead you?

4 In our culture, and perhaps to some degree in our churches too, there is a fear of other faiths. Their faith is easily portrayed as profane while ours is sacred. How might you mess with these dirt boundaries in a way that provokes good conversation?

Notes

1 Gina A. Zurlo, Todd M. Johnson and Peter F. Crossing, 'World Christianity and Mission 2020: Ongoing Shift to the Global South', in *International Bulletin of Missionary Research*, Vol. 44 (1), January 2020, p. 11.

2 Barbara Brown Taylor, *Holy Envy* (New York: HarperOne, 2019), p. 216.

3 Brown Taylor, *Holy Envy*, p. 216.

4 *CMS Newsletter*, No. 321, November 1968.

5 Ray Gaston, *Faith, Hope and Love: Interfaith Engagement as Practical Theology* (London: SCM Press, 2017), p. vii, quoted in Idina Dunmore, 'All are welcome here: the local church and radical hospitality in a multi-faith community', unpublished CMS MA dissertation, p. 9.

6 *CMS Newsletter*, No. 328, June 1969.

7 *CMS Newsletter*, No. 328.

8 *CMS Newsletter*, No. 345, January 1971.

9 *CMS Newsletter*, No. 345.

10 *CMS Newsletter*, No. 345.

11 *CMS Newsletter*, No. 303, April 1967.

12 *CMS Newsletter*, No. 303.

13 *CMS Newsletter*, No. 303.

14 *CMS Newsletter*, No. 382, June 1974.

15 *CMS Newsletter*, No. 382.

16 *CMS Newsletter*, No. 382.

17 *CMS Newsletter*, No. 382.

18 Travel Diaries, USA and Mexico 1963, p. 19.

19 John Taylor, *The Primal Vision* (London: SCM Press, 1963), pp. 105–6.

20 *CMS Newsletter*, No. 328, June 1969.

21 *CMS Newsletter*, No. 328.

22 *CMS Newsletter*, No. 328.

23 *CMS Newsletter*, No. 328.

24 *CMS Newsletter*, No. 328.

25 *CMS Newsletter*, No. 265, November 1963.

26 *CMS Newsletter*, No. 275, October 1964.

27 *CMS Newsletter*, No. 275.

28 Richard Rohr, quoted in Brown Taylor, *Holy Envy*, p. 217.

29 Stefan Paas, *Pilgrims and Priests, Christian Mission in a Post-Christian Society* (London: SCM Press, 2019), p. 209.

30 *CMS Newsletter*, No. 330, September 1969.

31 *CMS Newsletter*, No. 330.

32 *CMS Newsletter*, No. 330.

33 *CMS Newsletter*, No. 330.

34 *CMS Newsletter*, No. 330.

35 *CMS Newsletter*, No. 303, April 1967.

36 Travel Diaries, Pakistan, Nepal, Afghanistan, Russia, 1968, p. 107.

37 *CMS Newsletter*, No. 335, February 1970.

38 *CMS Newsletter*, No. 372, June 1973.

39 *CMS Newsletter*, No. 273, July 1964.

40 *CMS Newsletter*, No. 327, May 1969.

41 *CMS Newsletter*, No. 327.

42 Taylor, *The Primal Vision*, p. 16.

43 Kevin Colyer, from his assignment on Mission and Evangelism for a module as part of his CMS Pioneer Training. Used with permission.

44 *CMS Newsletter*, No. 327, May 1969.

45 Paas, *Pilgrims and Priests*, p. 104.

46 Paas, *Pilgrims and Priests*, p. 104.

47 *CMS Newsletter*, No. 376, December 1973.

48 *CMS Newsletter*, No. 376.

49 http://w2.vatican.va/content/francesco/en/apost_exhortations/documents/papa-francesco_esortazione-ap_20131124_evangelii-gaudium.html, paragraph 6.

50 *CMS Newsletter*, No. 284, July 1965.

51 *CMS Newsletter*, No. 284.

52 We are hugely indebted to Edward de Bono for the concept and language of provocations which he explores in Edward de Bono, *Teach Your Child to Think* (London: Penguin Books, 1993), p. 177–212. The roadblock analogy is reworked from his.

53 See de Bono, *Teach Your Child to Think*, p. 196; Robert Poynton's threefold improvisation approach does this too, Robert Poynton, *Do Improvise* (London: The Do Book Company, 2013), p. 15.

54 Brian Eno and Peter Schmidt, *Oblique Strategies*, first published 1975 – see www.enoshop.co.uk/product/oblique-strategies.html (accessed 3.3.2020).

55 Paul Arden, *Whatever You Think Think the Opposite* (London: Penguin Books, 2006).

56 de Bono, *Teach Your Child to Think*, p. 196.

57 de Bono, *Teach Your Child to Think*, p. 206.

58 Lewis Hyde, *Trickster Makes This World* (San Francisco, CA: North Point Press, 1999).

59 Mary Douglas explores this notion of dirt and dirt boundaries in *Purity and Danger* (London: Routledge, 1996).

60 Keith Johnstone, *Impro: Improvisation and Theatre* (London: Faber and Faber Ltd, 1979).

Outro

The Currency of Mission is Imagination

The biggest threat

We entitled this book *Imagining Mission* because our biggest takeway from encountering John Taylor through his newsletters is that he sparked our imagination afresh about mission. It is so refreshing to breathe air that is creative and imaginative and engenders in you a sense of wanting to try some new things and break some of the shackles in your own mind and practice. When Philip Mounstephen was interviewed at the point of leaving his role as the leader of Church Mission Society, he was asked to reflect on lessons that he had learned. The first thing he said in that interview was that mission is always a creative act, and then framing it the other way round, that the biggest threat to the Church in the West is a lack of imagination.[1] So by way of an outro to the book we offer a final reflection and reiterate that call to imagine.

You are creative

To be human is to be made in the image of God and one of the things that is particular to that image is the gift of imagination and creativity. We are all creative and imaginative. Of course, some are artists or designers and have cultivated that to a special degree, so we say that they have the gift of imagination or creativity. And indeed they do and it is a wonderful gift, but that notion quickly gets turned the other way round to say that we don't have the gift and therefore we are not creative. To say 'I'm not creative' is a block to creativity.[2] In a survey on the difference between those that met the criteria of being creative and those that didn't, one factor that was significant was that those who were creative thought they were creative! In other words, if we tell ourselves we're not creative it becomes a self-fulfilling prophecy! Rather than a gift, perhaps it might be more helpful to conceive of creativity as a muscle that is strengthened through use. It can go flabby if it is not exercised. We hope that the exercises at the end of each chapter provide a way into that exercise. So start telling yourself and your team or community that you are all creative!

The air we breathe

There are various teams, families or environments that we have known over the years where creativity is almost palpable. It's in the air, you feel as if you can catch it. We love being in those kinds of spaces. All of the children in a family are up to imaginative things, for example. That has always fascinated us – what is it about those environments? There is no dogma around creativity, but it's still celebrated. Ideas are played with, there is a curiosity, a sense of exploration and adventure. Stimulating books and music are just around. The food is often great too! When I first began youth ministry I was in a team that was led by someone who created that environment, or ecosystem, and as a team we used to talk about getting the creative juices flowing. It was so much fun. I don't think I would have self-described as creative back then, but breathing that air somehow helped me to think, 'Yes, I am creative'. Now, if people were asked to pick three words to describe me, 'imaginative' or 'creative' would be on most people's lists. John Taylor created that sort of ecosystem (if we may use that metaphor again) in CMS, created air that people in mission breathed in so that they perceived that mission is indeed a creative act, an adventure. How can we nurture these kinds of environments for churches, small groups, pioneer ministry, theological training colleges and courses, and mission organizations? Without repeating the arguments earlier in the book, this requires getting away from anxious and defended postures and becoming playful, discovering the freedom in the Spirit and the freedom that there is in Christ.

Learning from artists

As well as a foundational belief in being imaginative and nurturing environments where that is celebrated, the third thing we might pay attention to is the process of imagination. We love books on creativity, imagination and art. A game I sometimes play on my blog is to take a book that is intended for artists to reflect on and copy out some quotes but replace the word 'artist' with 'pioneer' or the word 'art' with 'mission'. This is because there is something about the processes of imagination and creativity that artists in particular have reflected on that has so much to teach us. Jeanette Winterson, for example, describes the currency of art as imagination, so we have taken to describing the currency of mission as imagination. She also says, 'Art is pushing at the boundaries we thought were fixed. The convenient lies fall; the only boundaries are the boundaries of our imagination. How much can we imagine? The artist is an imaginer.'[3] So we can say that pioneering is pushing at the boundaries we thought were fixed. The pioneer is an imaginer.

Or take Neil Gaiman's *Art Matters*, in which he says:

When you start out in [mission] you have no idea what you are doing. This is great. People who know what they are doing know the rules, and know what is possible and impossible. You do not. And you should not. If you don't know it's impossible it's easier to do. And because nobody's done it before, they haven't made up rules to stop anyone doing that again, yet.[4]

I have changed the word 'art' for 'mission'. In the chapter on training we reflected on how we have been inspired by books on art schools and the behaviours that make for flourishing artists and thought about the inspiring interplay between the internal characters 'hobbit' and 'punk'.

Immersion, imagination and improvisation

The process of creativity is described by Will Gompertz like this:

> Passion is the spur that makes us want to know more. It provides the impulse for the thoughtful enquiry that generates the knowledge which fires our imagination to come up with ideas. These lead to the experiments that eventually result in the production of a realised concept. That is the path that creativity takes.[5]

This is such a great description of the process of boundary-crossing mission, or what Taylor calls an adventure of the imagination. Three themes that recur in Taylor's reflections, and perhaps summarize his process, are immersion, imagination and improvisation. When we share Jesus Christ with someone in another culture there is a process of translation. This sounds straightforward but is actually a tricky art. The currency of this art, as we have said above, is imagination. That imagination involves a deep immersion in the Gospel, its stories and traditions out of which improvisation can take place.[6] The deeper the immersion, the richer the possibilities for improvisation will be because there is simply more to draw on. This process requires suspending our usual ways of doing things, ways in which our own imagination has been colonized by the forms of language and culture we are used to. It must address everything, letting go of preconceived notions and finding new ones that resonate with the local culture. This affects everything – what language is used to speak about God, how to open up prayer in and out of the experience of people's ordinary spirituality, what the Gospel is, what Church is, how life and faith would make sense in that community in ways that seem natural to the rhythms and forms of local culture, what materials from the tradition might be drawn on and remixed with local artefacts. It goes best when insiders to that culture become the carriers of the message. They are the ones who know their own language and culture best and can do it from the inside, as Taylor would say. All that is to say that if you are unsure how to develop creativity or imagination, pay attention to artists and creatives. In relation to how that plays out in mission, John Taylor has such wisdom for us to reflect on. We hope that you will try out some of the exercises at the end of each chapter in the book to get your creative juices flowing.

We have dedicated this book to the pioneers who have trained with us at CMS over the last decade. They have been and continue to be such an inspiration as they creatively join in with what God is doing in the world. Whether you are in youth ministry, a village, a housing estate, a multicultural district in a city, in the UK or on the other side of the world, we hope that this book has inspired you afresh to go on your own adventure of the imagination as you join in with God's creative Spirit who is at work in the world renewing all things, and as you share Jesus Christ who is the good news.

Notes

1 See Philip Mountstephen, 'The biggest threat to today's church? Lack of imagination', *Christian Today*, 21 November 2018, available from www.christiantoday.com/article/the-greatest-threat-to-todays-church-lack-of-imagination/130985.htm (accessed 16.1.2020).

2 Roger Von Oech, *A Whack on the Side of the Head* (New York, NY: Warner Books, 1983) has this as one of his mental blocks.

3 Jeanette Winterson, *Art Objects* (London: Vintage Books, 1996), p. 116.

4 Neil Gaiman, *Art Matters* (London: Headline Publishing Group, 2018), p. 54.

5 Will Gompertz, *Think Like an Artist* (London: Penguin, 2015), p. 60.

6 For more on this, see Jonny Baker and Ric Stott, 'I'll Meet You There: A Conversation on the Meeting Place of Mission and Imagination', in Cathy Ross and Colin Smith (eds), *Missional Conversations, A Dialogue between Theory and Praxis in World Mission* (London: SCM Press, 2018), pp. 192–201.

Index

Page numbers with n refer to notes. For example, 68n1 means note 1 on page 68. Roman numerals refer to pages in the *Intro*.